SYMBOLS

SYMBOLS
THEIR HISTORY, MEANING & EVOLUTION

ADELE NOZEDAR

SIRIUS

Images of The Sun and The Lovers tarot cards are in the public domain. All other images courtesy of Shutterstock.

This edition published in 2025 by Sirius Publishing, a division of Arcturus Publishing Limited,
26/27 Bickels Yard, 151–153 Bermondsey Street,
London SE1 3HA

Copyright © Arcturus Holdings Limited

All rights reserved. No part of this publication may be reproduced, stored in a retrieval system, or transmitted, in any form or by any means, electronic, mechanical, photocopying, recording or otherwise, without prior written permission in accordance with the provisions of the Copyright Act 1956 (as amended). Any person or persons who do any unauthorised act in relation to this publication may be liable to criminal prosecution and civil claims for damages.

ISBN: 978-1-3988-5226-6
AD011741UK

Printed in China

CONTENTS

INTRODUCTION 6

RELIGIOUS SYMBOLS 21

SYMBOLS OF LUCK, WEALTH AND POWER 37

MASONIC SYMBOLS AND RITUALS. 47

SYMBOLS OF THE OCCULT 53

GEMS AND STONES 63

SYMBOLS OF WITCHES 75

SYMBOLS OF DRUIDRY. 81

IMAGINARY ANIMALS 87

THE SYMBOLISM OF ANIMALS 97

OTHERWORLDLY ENTITIES. 111

THE WRITTEN WORD AND THE SPOKEN SOUND. . 117

SYMBOLS IN NATURE 123

CURIOSITIES. 145

INDEX 156

PICTURE CREDITS/ACKNOWLEDGEMENTS 160

INTRODUCTION

What exactly is a 'symbol'? A symbol is something that beyond its own reality represents something else, in particular a material object that represents an abstract concept. So, you could say that a diamond necklace is a symbol of wealth or that a coat of arms is a symbol of heritage or status.

Once you start to think about it, and as soon as you start to look, everything can become a symbol. For example, a tree can become a symbol of the natural world. Its blossoms can become a symbol of spring, the twirling leaves can be seen as a symbol of autumn and the fall. The type of tree also carries its symbols. The oak is a symbol of strength and endurance, and the acorn is a symbol of hope, especially when fallen on the ground and sprouting.

The actual word, 'symbol', is from the French, *symbole*, originally an ecclesiastical concept which morphed into something else and then evolved to the meaning of the word that we use today: 'a natural fact or object, evoking by its form or its nature an association of ideas with something abstract or absent.'

This introductory volume looks at some famous symbols as well as some more obscure ones, but once you begin to look for the symbolism inherent in everyday things, you will discover that it is everywhere. Although the meanings of symbols, in effect, do not change, the objects that we use, however inadvertently, to represent that meaning are definitely very different. Let's have a closer look at a car, an item that is often seen as a symbol, sometimes inextricably linked to the driver, and not only about the car itself. The driver's clothing, the kind of car, even its colour are all part of a symbolic whole. Next time you're in, say, a parking lot, take a moment to look around at those cars and their owners and see what you can discover. Often people will consciously choose their clothes and cars as symbols to represent who they are – or who they wish to be.

A POWERFUL SYMBOL... IN A PARKING LOT

Staying with the rich symbolism of cars, have you really looked at an Alfa Romeo? What do you know about this car already? At the very least you might guess that the owner is wealthy! If you look closer, though, you will see much more than you realize.

There's an interesting symbol, in the form of a badge, right at the front of the car. Because the car was built in Milan, the symbol is one of the city itself, the company incorporated in 1910.

The Alfa Romeo designers have used the crest of the House of Visconti, a noble Italian family (still extant). The crest is seen above the Archbishop's Palace in Milan. In using this symbol, the car itself is embued with some of the glitter of the dynasty, which goes back to the 11th century.

The badge also features two halves of a circle. The left part in deference to the red cross that was worn by the Milanese soldiers during the era of the Crusades – more noble history. The cross, while it looks like St George's Cross, is actually the Cross of St Ambrose and is the flag of the city of Milan. St Ambrose was the Bishop of the City, and his cross was literally pinned to a sacred wagon, ready for battle. Rather like a car, perhaps?

The serpent that can be seen on the badge is, again, in honour of the Visconti dynasty. This is an interesting symbol, a snake with a man in its mouth called a *Biscione*. The translation of this is 'big grass snake' or 'Vipera' or else, simply, a 'beast'. Here we see an example of heraldry in action. The symbol is called a 'charge', an emblem on a shield. This particular charge and its provenance suggest two potential meanings. One story tells us that the serpent is in the act of giving birth to a child. Other sources say that the snake is eating the person whole. It's highly unlikely that we will ever know the truth, but then that's all part of the intrigue of symbols.

A further heraldic symbol of knots used to divide the names of 'Alfa' and 'Romeo' on the logo of the car's border. This was used in the heraldry of Milan, too, but these knots were removed in the 1950s.

There was also a four-leafed clover badge added to the high-performance model of the car, placed in 1923 in homage to four of the

car's designers. These clovers, of course, are symbols of good luck in Mediterranean, European and western North America.

The name, Alfa Romeo, is a beautiful blend of serendipity. A.L.F.A is the acronym for 'Anonima Lombarda Fabbrica Automobili'. The word, Alpha, as in Alpha Male, could be a symbolic reminder of the sort of person who, we might suppose, could be exactly the right choice for such a car.

A ROSE BY ANY OTHER NAME

And how about one more, very different symbol to whet your appetite? What about… a rose?

Arguably a queen among flowers, and a symbol of love in many languages. It is easy to forget that the rose, now seen as a pretty garden ornament, was on this planet a long time before we can imagine, some 35 million years ago. It should be no surprise, then, that these fragrant blossoms with their vicious thorns, sharp enough to draw blood, have a tale to tell.

In India, for example, a rose is carefully shed of its thorns, snapped off from the stem, before offering them as a gift of love or respect. In Rome, roses were painted on the walls and ceilings of banqueting rooms as a reminder not to spill secrets after drinking too much wine. In the same way, the symbol of a rose on a confessional was a sign that anything said was private. The 15th century Wars of the Roses in England was a bloody series of battles that took some thirty years before peace reigned again. As a marker of this accord, the White Rose of Yorkshire was amalgamated with the Red Rose of Lancashire, the emerging symbol called the Tudor Rose, still seen today.

A red rose is not just a pretty flower, but is also an offer of sexual love, seen on Valentine's Day, hawkers loaded with buckets of the long red stems. The white rose, whilst pure, also has connotations of female sexuality, particularly in the scented varieties.

The idea of symbols, their meanings and their usefulness, does not change. However, the symbols themselves adapt continually without forgetting their previous iterations.

Red Rose of Lancaster   *Tudor Rose*   *White Rose of York*

In terms of the rose, we could hybridise it, change its colour, the shape of its leaves and even its scent. But it is still a rose.

ESSENTIAL BASIC SYMBOLS

Where it comes to symbols, nothing is really 'basic' in the true sense of the word. But the following lists and descriptions are certainly that which most of us would recognise as such. The first of these symbols is, literally, nothing – and also everything. In fact, it is true to say that the simpler the symbol, the more scope there is for interpretation, hence the more mysterious and meaningful it becomes. You may think these 'basic' shapes are so self-explanatory as to merit no further analysis. To do this would be a mistake. These shapes are the bedrock of symbolism. Think of them in the same way that a painter needs to prime his canvas, or a singer needs to tune up. These symbols appear again and again, in alchemy, the zodiac, numerology, the tarot, freemasonry, runic symbols and more.

Space

Think of 'space' as something that is defined by what is not there. That can be tricky to get your head around. Like the wind, the effect of space is noted by what surrounds it, or what is in it. The concept of a 'void' is a deep part of our experience. For some, the concept of 'emptiness' is, ultimately, a spiritual experience. To reach such a state, for some, is to connect with the Absolute. The possibility of space, within a flat two-dimensional representation, is to give the shape some substance, in the same way that you – the reader – is part of this page, right now, as you read. Zero is a space. The fact that 'nothing' can morph into 'something' was a huge step in our human intelligence.

Dot

This little symbol might not seem significant – but look again! When we write, the 'dot' tells us when the writing is complete. The dot is also a beginning, the first mark on an otherwise pristine sheet of paper. The dot has at least two uses, as a beginning and an end. It also tells us where the arms of a cross intersect. Hindu faith uses a specific mark – a dot or *bindhu* – as a symbol of the Absolute, a marker of the Third Eye, said to be the seat of the soul. As an embellishment around the door of a temple, the dot is of significance to worshipers, such as the Jain Symbol, which features three dots, a reminder of the Three Tenets of Jainism. Similarly, the two dots of the yin-yang symbol are a reminder of two halves, representing opposing forces.

Circle

The circle is an extrapolation, or expansion, of the dot. It represents the Cosmos. Like the dot, the circle is also made of 'some thing' and 'no thing'. The circle connects spirit and matter. A circle has no beginning and no end and, because of this, it is unassailable and is used in magical practice as a 'fortress' of psychic protection. Nature gives us natural circles, such as the Sun and the Moon, both masculine and feminine at different times, the stars in their orbits. The circle symbolises unity throughout all of creation. Sacred circles comprise the four directions, sometimes with a fifth (Spirit or Ether) added. The Knights of the Round Table, with an equal space around the table of King Arthur, is a symbol of the egalitarian status of the knights of Arthur's realm.

Arc

Possibly the best instance of a natural arc is that of a rainbow, perfectly symmetrical, impossible to touch no matter how hard we try. In many cultures, including the Navajo, the rainbow is seen as a bridge between Heaven and Earth. This can also

suggest a bridge between the feminine and masculine. If held upright, like a chalice, it traditionally symbolised the feminine (water, mother, gentleness), whereas if it is inverted, it traditionally became a masculine symbol (war, victory, triumph). The vaulted, arched shape of many holy buildings, no matter where in the world they are or which religion they are dedicated to, represents the great vault of the heavens. As part of a circle, the Arc can suggest the potential of Spirit.

Vertical Line and Horizontal Line

The horizontal line is a very simple symbol on the face of it. The horizontal line tells of matter (rather than spirit) and the forward and backward movement of time. It also symbolises the horizon, and our place on the Earth as human beings. Because the human is the only animal that stands upright, we are associated with the vertical line, the number one, and the concept of striving towards spirit. The tree, too, as the World Tree or *Axis Mundi* (a line or stem through the centre of the earth, connecting its surface to the underworld and the heavens in which the Universe revolves) is connected to spirit. The vertical line is the most basic of phallic symbols, also symbolising the union with the Divine. This simple upright tells us precisely in any given moment where we are. It also symbolises strength, vitality, potency and potential.

Cross

Here, the vertical and horizontal lines come together to make a new symbol – the Cross. The earliest example of this symbol, ancient beyond reckoning, possibly originated from ancient Babylon. The Cross is a symbol of protection par excellence as well as being a useful sign with many interpretations. Because of its convergence of vertical and horizontal lines, it speaks of the union of both material and spiritual. And, because of its four cardinal points, it symbolises the elements and the directions. In geometry (sacred or secular alike), if you put a cross inside a circle, the circle can be equally divided. Because of this, the circle is said to 'give birth' to the square. Cross-shaped icons of all kinds can be seen in all corners of the globe, that idea of protection universal to us all.

Square

This is said to be the first shape ever 'invented' by mankind. Whether or not this is true, the business-like square generally represents the more spiritual and natural dimensions of the circle. The square, clearly, represents the Earth and the four elements and, although the saying 'four corners of the earth' is clearly a nonsense because the earth is round, nevertheless we still use the analogy. Whereas a circle is in constant motion, the square is safe: static and reliable, and sometimes unfairly called boring. Temples are usually built in squares, designed to line up with the points of the compass. In churches, the altar is a solid oblong, and the Ka'aba at Mecca is a good example of a huge and imposing example. A square holds boundaries in a way that a circle cannot do, sometimes rigid and unyielding, but clear in its stability.

Lozenge

A symbol that seems to be overlooked, the lozenge is in fact a representation of female genitalia. The motif, it is believed, dates from the Neolithic and Paleolithic ages in the general area of Eastern Europe. It is said to look like a sown field as an image for fertility. You might have seen similar diamond shapes on the dress patterns and embroidery of Ukraine. Also known as a 'rhombus', this fertility symbol can also be seen in carpet designs as well as in amulets. In a pack of cards, the Diamond suit is a lozenge too. The symbol of the Vesica Piscis, which is Latin, means 'fish bladder', is frequently to be seen in the oval-shaped images of the Christ, usually depicted holding out his hands. This symbolizes the Virgin, the Mother Goddess (for Pagans), and Her womb.

Triangle

The shape of the triangle is a reminder, if we ever needed one, of the strength and mystery of the number 3, wrapped up in a shape. Therefore this symbol represents the ideas and concepts that come in threes. These include the Holy Trinity, the Triple Goddess, the Triskele symbol, clover leaves, and many more. The triangle was, once upon a time, associated with light and this idea is seen in the rays of light emanating from the US dollar bill, aka the 'All Seeing Eye of God'. The shape of this symbol is both strong and also flexible, a shape that can vary depending on which way up it is. On its base it is a solid – virile, masculine – representing the notion of fire. Inverted, it becomes the feminine principle such as the shape of a bowl or chalice and represents water.

Diagonal

Because a square can be divided into two diagonal triangles, and also because the length of the two shapes has no simple relationship to its sides, it was concluded by the ancient Greeks that the diagonal must be a symbol of the irrational. Also called an oblique, because of the unusual and contrary shape, it is often associated with matters of an occult nature. Diagonal lines and shapes are more dynamic than a simpler shape, hence a feeling of movement, potential energy, and a sense of uncertainty. J.K Rowling, who imagined and wrote the Harry Potter books, used this to great effect in Diagon Alley, a place that is notoriously tricky to find even when the protagonists have been there many times before. Some film directors, such as Alfred Hitchcock, deliberately used diagonal lines to accentuate a feeling of menace or disturbance.

Zig-Zag

Heat, energy, movement, vitality are all part of the zigzag. The origins of the word itself are not clear, but the shape is ancient, even found in caves of the Palaeolithic Age (which ended around 15,000- 10,000 BCE). We don't know the actual significance of these zig-zag cave paintings although some scientists believe that they might have had a protective or magical purpose. It has been posited that the symbol might be a picture of a snake, such as a viper. The dorsal zig-zag line certainly looks like one, and this snake is still one of the most common, found in Europe and Asia. The symbol was first noted in print in 17th century French, possibly in describing mountainous hairpin bends. In the natural world we find the symbol in the form of lightning bolts. It is also seen as an architectural motif in Islamic, Byzantine, Norman and Romanesque buildings and temples. In sewing or embroidery, the zig-zag is used to strengthen seams, giving the symbol a similar underlying idea of strength and resilience, too.

RELIGIOUS SYMBOLS

There are countless ways in which human beings have expressed the idea of an overriding force that looks after us, and this expression is seen in the clothes that are worn, the songs that are sung, and the stories that are told. The religions and faiths of billions of people on this planet are, arguably, a source of many of our ideas about the planet and the people on it. For this reason, there is a deliberate emphasis on this subject when we examine symbols.

Altar

An altar is a high place, a holy place, and the symbol of a mountain. The word comes from the Latin, *altarium* meaning 'high', as well as *adolere*, to 'ritually burn or sacrifice' which is a reminder of a less kind version of religious worship. An altar is raised up from its surroundings, a focus of holy rites and sacred practices. The concept is the same all over the world, no matter the religion. Altars, and those who tend them, as well as the sacred vessels used – Chalice (cup), Paten (plate) and Ciborium (a covered container) – have to be sparklingly clean before the rites commence.

Ark

An 'ark' is a vessel (as in a ship or boat) that affords protection and safety. In this instance it is the Ark of the Covenant, a sacred relic in the shape of a chest believed to contain the Tablets of the Law or the Ten Commandments. The Ark was created according to the pattern that God gave to Moses when the Israelites were encamped at the foot of Mount Sinai. Instructions as to its making included using acacia wood as a base, the entire Ark to be gilded (including a crown), with four golden rings attached to the corners. Staves of acacia wood, also gilded, were added to aid carrying the Ark. The staves must never be removed.

I H S

These initials form a symbolic monogram for the Christ. It comprises the Greek letters *iota*, *ete* and *sigma*, the first three letters of the name of Jesus (or Iesous). The letters also stand for a further phrase, in Latin, 'Iesus Hominum Salvator', which means 'Jesus, Saviour of Man'. Later, the symbol became a sign of peace. The symbol is usually embossed onto the communion wafer, the initials surrounded by the rays of the Sun to represent the light of Christ.

Chi-Rho

Dating back to the very early days of Christianity, this is the fusion of the Greek letter *chi* and *rho*, which, when put together, form the first two letters of the Greek word for 'Christ'. Today, we often see this symbol in churches, specifically those of the Catholics. In the same way that the ichthys was used as a secret sign, so the Chi-Rho was used in the same way. These signs, prevalent during the time when it was dangerous to be Christian, are called 'Christograms'. Pictured here is the Chi-Rho between the letters alpha and omega.

The Khanda

This symbol is from the Sikh religion. It symbolises the four aspects of the Faith, as well as encompassing the four sacred weapons that sit within the shape. The Khanda is a double-edged sword that sits in the centre of the symbol. It signifies the creative power of God, and the knowledge of divinity. The circle around the edge of the symbol is called the 'chakkar' (or wheel) and shares the same root as the word 'chakra'. As in circular symbols the world over, this represents eternity and unification. At the side of the symbol, crossing at the base, are Kirpans, yet more symbols. These knives were worn by Guru Hargobind, sixth of the ten gurus of the Sikh faith, and they symbolise the balance of matter (*miri*) and spirit (*piri*).

Swastika

This is an ancient Sun Symbol, so old that it may have been in use as far back as Palaeolithic times. It is seen the world over, including as a symbol within Hinduism in India and Nepal. Thailand, China, Japan, Sri Lanka and also the Navajo people of the Southwest USA have their own versions of this symbol. Tragically, it was appropriated, notoriously, by the German Nazi Party, and is still used by neo-nazis. The word itself, *swastika*, means, among other interpretations, 'to be conducive to well-being'. Facing clockwise the sign symbolises the Sun, prosperity and good luck. Facing counterclockwise, it symbolises the opposite, including the destructive aspects of the Goddess Kali, who wears a necklace of skulls around her neck.

Sri Yantra

This Hindu symbol – whose design was inspired by sacred geometry – is formed of nine interlocking triangles which, together, make the pattern. Put together, they represent the totality of the Cosmos and also express the tenets of non-duality (also called Advaita). This is a form of a mystical diagram, a tantric ritual drawing, that is used as an aid to meditation and concentration. Often

drawn or used as a metal talisman, in order to use the symbol correctly, the Sri Yantra is set facing the rising sun, in a calm place bereft of clutter so that it is easier to meditate upon. It can be worn as a pendant as a reminder of the power of the Cosmos and our place within it.

Rudraksha

Within Hinduism, this is a necklace or pendant made from the dried seeds of the rudraksha tree, whose botanical name is *elaeocarpus ganitrus*. It is found in many parts of the world as well as in India, including Australia and Hawaii. The seeds have a naturally-occurring blue colouration as well as a differing number of 'faces' or 'facets' which look like segments. These facets are more or less magical, with a single stone being the rarest and therefore most sought-after. Other 'special' seeds include eleven facets belonging to renunciants, a seed of two faces makes for a married couple, and one with five faces symbolises the monkey god, Hanuman. The necklace is often used as a garland or mala.

Murti

This a devotional image in Hinduism, meaning 'an embodiment', and it is an effigy of a god or, more likely, 'gods'. The murti is a symbolic icon that represents the Divinity for the purposes of devotional activities. A 'murti' is not a god or goddess, but rather a reminder, representative shape or iconic representation of the deity. They are made in numerous different media, such as stone, metalwork and pottery, showing different depictions of the characters portrayed. They are used in domestic homes as well as in temples, treated as gods, and given water, sweets and incense in worship.

Yorishiro

In Shintoism, which is a religion that originates in Japan, the natural world is paramount. It is polytheistic, believing in, or worshiping, many gods including the supernatural powers that exist in the natural world. Spirits, called 'kami', reside in all kinds of places such as stones, plants, features of the landscape (mountains, rivers, etc.) people and even the dead. A yorishiro houses kami and are often surrounded by ropes called *shimenawa* and decorated with *shide*, paper streamers, to indicate their sacredness.

Druze Star

The Druze people, and faith, are a group in west Asia of an Arabic-speaking esoteric faith. They are Abrahamic, and believe in God, the eternity of the soul, and reincarnation. Their religious practices are generally kept a secret. They do not allow outsiders to convert to the religion, and marriage outside of the faith is rare. The central tenets of their faith are laid out in a text called *The Epistles of Wisdom*. At the centre of this is the emphasis on the mind and the truth. The Druze believe that at the end of the cycle of rebirth, achieved by successive reincarnations, the Soul is united with the Cosmic Mind. While they strictly eschew iconography, they do use five colours to represent the five 'limits' or metaphysical powers. These colours are green for the Universal Mind or Intelligence, Red for Universal Soul, Yellow for The Word, Blue for the First Intellect and white for The Effect. The Druze Star shows this and is often found on their places of worship.

Yazidi Peacock Angel

The religion of the Yazidi people absorbs elements of ancient Iranian religions as well as elements of Judaism, Christianity and Islam. They are a Kurdish minority, numbering only approximately 200,000 people. Their mythology suggests that they were created separately from the rest of mankind, descended from Adam, but not from Eve. As such, they are endogamous, meaning that they must marry within their community. Their creation story is particularly fascinating. A supreme creator god constructed the world, then handed it over to the control of seven divine beings. The chief of these is Malak-Ta'us, the Peacock Angel, worshipped in the form of the bird. Outsiders identified this as Satan, which meant that they were described, erroneously, as worshippers of the devil. Their worship is symbolized by bronze or iron effigies known as *sanjaqs*, circulated from town to town. Once there were seven of these effigies, but now it is thought that only two still exist.

Fulu

A traditional symbol of Taoist magical symbols and incantations (see opposite), which, in English, translates as a 'talismanic script'. The talisman is drawn onto cloth as a protective force. Early iterations of this talisman were simple and easy to read; however, as they developed, the Taoist priests made the talismans more and more deliberately cryptic, a mark of their divinity. The illegibility itself became a marker of supernatural provenance.

Tao Symbol

Commonly known as the Yin-Yang symbol and otherwise known as the *Ta Ki*, this popular symbol has extended throughout the world. Two identical shapes fit snugly inside a circle, making two S shapes, identical apart from one being black and the other, white. The shape of the Yin-Yang represents the interplay and interaction of opposing forces, *yin* as female and *yang* as male; *yin* is moon energy – cold, passive, female – whereas *yang* is the Sun, heat, action and male.

Supreme Polarity Symbol

Although the Yin-Yang symbol is common, the Supreme Polarity symbol is generally lesser-known, at least in the West. The symbol effectively explains the Yin-Yang symbol in a more three-dimensional way. The primary concept of Taoism is the Tao, meaning the 'path' or 'the way', and encompasses three aspects. These are the Way of Reality, the Way of Nature, and The Way of Human Life. The primary goal of life, for a Taoist, is to align oneself with the Tao.

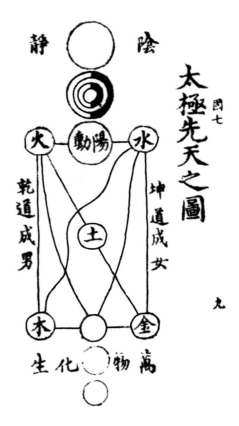

Yantra

In Buddhism and Hinduism, the Yantra is a linear geometric figure that embodies a spoken chant or mantra, effectively, in a symbol. Further, the symbol is a symbol of the Cosmos, and the drawing of the symbol and the contemplating of it goes back over 2,000 years ago, the Hindu equivalent of the Buddhist mandala. It is used as a focus for concentration and meditation, containing further symbolic meaning within the design. These include triangles, pointed upwards for male energy, or downwards for female energy.

The Laughing Buddha

Called 'Hotei' or 'Budai' in China, this statuette is seen in the reception areas of hotels, workplaces and restaurants as well as in the home, particularly in places of Chinese origin. He is plump, with a gregarious grin, holding or sitting on various objects including a string of prayer beads, a fan, a bowl and a large sack; all these are symbols of abundance. This jovial person has various poses, including standing in welcome, sitting and laughing, and with a bowl, symbolic of abundance and generosity. His origins are said to be of a real person, loved by everyone in the town, especially children. He was able to predict fortunes and the weather. He is also part of a group called the Seven Lucky Gods, based in Japanese mythology. Be aware that a statue of this figure needs the correct alignment according to the rules of feng shui. Also, be aware that this Buddha is not the Gautama Buddha!

SYMBOLS OF LUCK, WEALTH AND POWER

Do you believe that certain objects are able to alter the pattern of your life, simply because they are said to be lucky? Or do you think that this is just plain silly?

Even as we are laughing at ourselves, an older, less rational mindset is hard to shake off and, what's more, there is a useful psychological benefit in superstition. Within reason, a sense of security and confidence can come from some superstitious practices – for example, wearing a particular colour or an object that is found to be soothing, when you are going for an interview. In fact, psychologists at the University of Cologne discovered that invoking good-luck related superstitions (such as crossing fingers) actually made applicants feel more confident and able.

The Beckoning Cat

Also called Maneki-neko, its welcoming, beckoning pose is not dissimilar in effect from the Laughing Buddha, and it has a tranche of differing stories to match. The best-known of these is from 1622–24 CE. Legend has it that the priest of a small Buddhist temple had befriended a stray cat. One day a group of samurai passed by, noting that the cat looked as though it was beckoning to them. As they stopped to say hello, the heavens opened to a colossal thunderstorm, with lightning strikes to boot. The samurai believed that the cat had saved them, and the story of the cat became a legend, its effigy found far and wide. Like the Laughing Buddha, the cat symbolizes a series of different aspects according to what her paws are doing.

Horseshoe

Why would a rusty old iron horseshoe be considered such a lucky symbol? There is never a single answer to such questions, but it could be due to the coming of the age of iron. The fairy folk, witches and the like simply do not like iron. Before it came, the world was quieter and calmer. But, as progress marched onwards, those that were afraid of iron retreated. Iron is a sort of kryptonite for otherworldly beings. Given that most humans find the fairy folk frightening, the horseshoe was hammered onto doors to ward away the unmentionable. So, the Lucky Horseshoe became a symbol not only of good luck, but also of protection.

Lucky Chimney Sweep

Why is it that the chimney sweep symbolizes good luck, even at a wedding where the bride might be wearing a snowy white dress? And why should it be that if the sweep kisses the bride then it is even luckier? And that in Germany, Austria, Hungary and other countries they are considered a lucky omen if you see him on New Year's Day? It might be because the sweep removes the grubby old detritus from the chimney, making everything clean and safe against fires. In addition, King George III of England was saved by a chimney sweep calming his bolting horse. Thereafter, the chimney sweep became a symbol of good luck, by tradition and royal decree.

Four-leafed Clover

For many, the pinnacle of good luck is the four-leafed clover. There are also, on occasion, even luckier specimens than the four-leafed; five-, six- and seven-leafed specimens have been found around the planet. This description, from 1869, observed that '*four-leafed clovers gathered at night time during the full moon by sorceresses, who mixed it with vervain and other ingredients, whilst young girls in search of a token of happiness made quest of the plant by day*'. It is the rarity value that makes this little plant fortunate for those that find it; in addition, it looks very much like the shamrock, a good-luck token popularly found in Ireland as well as in other wooded places where some believe the fairies dance. The car maker Alfa Romeo uses the four-leafed clover as a symbol of success.

Hamsa

The hamsa or *khamsa* (which means 'five' in Arabic) is a symbol used throughout the Middle East and North Africa. It represents spiritual protection – particularly from the evil eye – as well as myriad blessings and good fortune. Typically shown as a hand with three extended fingers in the middle and two on either side, it is often associated with the Hand of Fatima in Islamic tradition or the Hand of Miriam in Jewish culture. The idea of the evil eye or a jealous, negative influence is present in almost every country of the world and is a very ancient belief. This symbol is often worn or displayed to ensure divine protection and guidance in combatting the tyranny of the evil eye.

Eye of Ra

The eye of Ra is a fascinating and potent symbol from ancient Egypt. It is the female counterpart to the Sun god and was able to leave his body to use its potency to punish transgressors and empower goddesses such as Sekhmet and Hathor. The teardrop that is often seen under the eye is said to be the source of the first people and, in some stories, of all life on Earth, hinting at the eye's powers of fertility and growth. It was worn as an amulet to repel evil and was often carved atop doors to ensure protection for those who resided inside. This was also the case with funerary objects as the eye was said to protect the soul on its journey in the afterlife. Its dual purpose of protection and punishment echoes in the power of the Sun, which can both give and destroy life.

SYMBOLS OF LUCK, WEALTH AND POWER

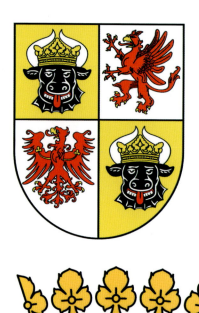

HERALDRY

In the realms of heraldry, the Knights and their families were Norman, and spoke Norman French. This is why 'heralds' still use this language to describe coats of arms. These coats of arms, which are still in use, originated with the need to be able to identify opposing armies as well as single combatants. The language of these ancient symbols has been used for almost a thousand years, although soldiers of much earlier times painted images, personal to themselves, not only so that they could be recognised in battle but also as a talisman. Here is not an exhaustive study of the often-elaborate heraldic codes, but a general overview of some of the most commonly used emblems. Each heraldic shield was personal to the wearer and held in high esteem. The colours used are generally bright, strong and easy to see.

SYMBOLS OF LUCK, WEALTH AND POWER

Heraldry Tinctures

The colours of heraldry are called 'tinctures'. There are also patterns called 'furs'. The most common ones are:

Ermine (representing the white winter fur of stoats, with their distinctive black tail tips).

Vair (representing squirrel skins, in blue and white).

If an animal (such as a dog, or a badger) is shown in its natural colours, this is called 'proper'.

Here are the names of the colours as they were used in the Norman French era, and are still used today.

Red – Gules	Green – Vert	Silver – Argent
Blue – Azure	Purple – Purpure	Gold – Or
	Black – Sable	

So that the colours are sure to be clearly seen, one colour is very rarely laid on top of another. The same rule applies to the metallic colours (that is, to gold or silver).

Charges

This is, effectively, a symbolic picture. This image can be, for example, a geometric design, a plant, a real animal, or an imaginary animal, such as a dragon or a unicorn (we look at some of these mythical beasts on pages 86-95).

It might be surprising to know that is not only men that have heraldic shields – women have them too. Since women did not go to war, specific heraldic designs are shown on a lozenge-type framework (like a diamond shape tipped on its side) instead of the shield shape of the male. The lozenge shape is suggestive of the *vesica piscis*, a feminine symbol. Similarly, non-combative members of the clergy also used the lozenge or oval shape.

SYMBOLS OF LUCK, WEALTH AND POWER

MASONIC SYMBOLS AND RITUALS

Although the origins of the Freemasons are by definition full of secrets, many of the symbols of the craftsman are also used by them. At the core of this venerable institution is the legend of Hiram Abiff, a master mason who specialised in metalwork. Abiff was, so the story goes, one of the most regarded designers of the Temple of Solomon in Jerusalem. Some of the other workers, jealous of Hiram's expertise, demanded to know his secrets. When the master mason refused, the hoodlums killed him. Full of remorse, they buried him under an acacia tree. Latter day masons re-enact the tale as part of their initiatory rites.

Column

The symbols of Freemasonry are inspired from the Temple of Solomon. The Hall has two columns at either side of the main door that relate to the Hiram's brief that the columns be set in the porch of the Temple. The pillars are known by their Hebrew names, also referred to in the Jewish mystical tradition, the Kabbalah. On the right is Jachin, meaning 'stability' and on the left is Boaz, meaning 'strength'. Jachin is often painted in red, to symbolise the force of the Sun, and Boaz, the feminine principle, painted white to resemble the Moon. You can also see these columns in the High Priestess card on the Rider-Waite-Smith tarot deck (see page 58).

Level and Plumbline

Again, these inseparable practical tools are embued with a deeper symbolic meaning. The level comprises a set square, from which hangs the plumbline. These tools can define both vertical and horizontal lines, a reminder of the Cross of the Christ. The saying, 'on the level' (which means something that is honest and true) is a direct descendant of the philosophical meaning of the word.

Triangle

For Freemasons, this triangle symbolises the Greek capital, A, also known as the 'Shining Delta'. Also, the triangle indicates the meanings of objects or concepts in triplicate, such as 'right thinking, right speaking, right doing'. One of the most famous examples of this is the Masonic Triangle, which also includes a Blazing Star as seen on the Seal of the United States and on the United States Dollar (see opposite).

The Bride's Chair

(also known as the 47th Problem of Euclid)

One of the foundations of freemasonry, this mathematical theorem is given the name for no other reason that it was the 47th problem of the mathematical book written by Euclid. Put simply, this is a measuring device. Also known as the Egyptian String Trick, a practical demonstration in the making of a shape that illustrates its efficacy perfectly. Take a piece of string and tie 12 knots at exact intervals along the string. Then join the ends of the string ensuring once more that the intervals are perfect. Then, hammer a stick into the ground. Put one of the knots over the stick. Stretch three divisions of knots, then take another stick and skewer it into the ground at the point of the fourth knot. This will give a triangle in the proportions of three, four and five, and further, the lines of string can be extrapolated to make three squares of 9 parts, 16 parts, and 15 parts.

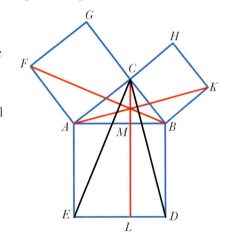

52 ❖ SYMBOLS

The United States Dollar Bill

If you are ever without a book to read – in an airport, for example – have a look at the United States Dollar Bill instead. This note (a symbol in itself) is cluttered with further symbols, full of arcane imagery, a wonderful example of symbolism in action. Although the design of the bill has altered through time, nevertheless most of the elements have remained constant. There are many conspiracy theories too, but to read the bill is to imagine a group of men simply doing their best to make their resolutions meaningful.

On the reverse if the Great Seal of the United States, taking the form of a pyramid with the 'cap' sliced off to be replaced by a triangle with an eye inside; this is the All-Seeing Eye. The phrase 'Annuit Coeptus', written around the top of the seal, means 'we favour the things which have begun', indicating that there is more to come. The use of latin gives gravity to the Bill, and a feeling of ancient wisdom. The Bald Eagle appears as the bird symbol of the USA. It holds the olive branch, an ancient symbol of peace, but also has arrows clutched in its grasp. Although there is a further symbol of the USA , a dove, it does not take part on the Dollar Bill. There is said to be an owl secreted on the note, too. A superb symbol of secrecy, it is almost impossible to find. Finally, there is a crown of 13 stars. These represent the 13 states that first joined the Union. The saying, 'out of many comes one', refers to the many states that originally formed the Union.

MASONIC SYMBOLS AND RITUALS ❖ 53

SYMBOLS OF THE OCCULT

Any good book about symbols, and anyone interested in the subject, will be intrigued by occult symbols, and rightly so. But what does 'occult' actually mean, and is the concept still valid? The word itself means 'hidden' but it has come to mean supernatural or mystical beliefs and rituals.

As human beings adapted, and we started to work out how the world worked, we began to wonder about the nature of hidden or secret things. Many of these secrets, though, are hidden in plain sight. No matter how sophisticated we are, we are still intrigued by the secret, the hidden, and the ambiguous. Remember that western symbolism is far younger than Eastern, and that many of 'our' symbols once belonged to another age entirely.

THE TAROT

Believed to be a set of symbols linked to various mystery traditions such as the Kabbalah and Alchemy, the tarot emerged in Italy, sometime in the early 1430s, specifically from around Milan and Florence. Initially known as 'tarocci', the cards were used as a game; the present-day association with the tarot as a way of fortune-telling did not emerge until the 19th century, something which people generally don't realise. It was French occultists, it is believed, that made elaborate (but erroneous) claims about the divinatory qualities of the cards. Carl Jung noticed that the cards, with their realistic and differing types of humanity, in deftly categorised stages and kinds of humanity, so much more than a fortune-telling device.

We do not have space in this book for all of the cards so I have randomly chosen four cards of the Major Arcana as an example of this intriguing 'game'.

The Sun – Number 9

Twin figures, looking very much like children, a boy and a girl, bask in the rays of the sun, whose rays fall to the earth. These 'twins' are also a symbol of one of the astrological signs, too – Gemini. The Sun is a 'happy' card, heralding the dawning of a new day full of optimism and freshness. The children play in the full light of day, safely bounded by the solidity of the material world in the form of a wall. These are a symbol of Adam and Eve, in their state of innocence before they ate the Fruit of Wisdom. This tarot card is a signifier of harmony, happiness, a promise fulfilled and the moment of the completion that defines enlightenment.

The Lovers – Number 6

This card is sometimes misread. Although there are three characters, only one of these is actually the Lover. Traditionally, this is a man, who has to

decide which of the two women he prefers. but there is no reason that two men, or two women, or a combination, should not be depicted. The card itself, whatever the gender, is about choices. The character shows an ordinary person, with no mystical attributes, faced with a time-worn dilemma. Above the head is Cupid, ready to strike with his bow and arrow. This is a symbol that the hapless human has nothing to do with the choices that he thinks he is making; he is a simply a puppet of the powers of destiny.

The World – Number 21

This is the final card of the Major Arcana, which symbolizes the coming of age, and when, symbolically, a key is given on his or her 21st birthday. The depiction of this card is of a young woman whose veil or scarf covers at least a little of her modesty. She holds wands in both her hands, symbolizing completion. The card also shows four creatures, called 'tetramorphs', which are human or hybrid creatures that rule over the elements and the four corners of the earth. The character is surrounded by a garland of laurel, a symbol of victory, shaped like a *vesica piscis*. She emerges from this symbol as though from the spiritual world to the material one. The tetramorphs are not only the witnesses of her new-found status but also a symbol of the four corners of the world, which are now hers. The pair of wands imply the perfect balance of opposites– matter and spirit – and the harmony of the Universe.

The High Priestess – Number 2

Also called the Popess, the number 2, historically, is the number of the female. She stands between the two pillars associated with the Temple of Solomon, in their turn an influential design of Masonic temples. The scroll is symbolic of wisdom, as well as the secrets of the Universe. The card shows a veil, which tells us that secrets are revealed, certainly, but only to the initiate. The crown shows heavenly authority, and the throne, earthly power. In some representations of the Priestess, she appears with three parts to her crown. This is a hidden reminder of the triple aspect of the Moon, in its three phases – new, full and waning. The Priestess also symbolises the notion of balance between opposing forces.

KABBALAH

This is a huge and labyrinthine topic, a deeply mystical and enigmatic aspect of the Jewish doctrine. As is the case in many mystery traditions, its secrets were passed orally, rather than written down. The word, 'Cabal' means 'secret intrigue'. There are many aspects to this fascinating subject. It has an external level of understanding used for the general multitude, and also a more esoteric meaning reserved for the Priests. These secrets are said to have been given directly from God, thence to the Archangels, and thence to Adam, after he and Eve were expelled from the Garden of Eden. Then the secrets were passed on to Noah, then to Abraham, then to the Egyptians. From the Egyptians, the mysteries spread to other parts of the planet. The influence of the Kabbalah is wide-ranging, influencing, amongst other disciplines, the tarot, Freemasonry, Rosicrucianism and more. Here we have just a few snippets from which you can delve deeper.

The Four Worlds

IHVH is a sort of shorthand for the Greatest Name, that is, Jehovah. The letters also stand for the concept of the Four Worlds.

Atziluth which means 'emanation', a world of spirit, and the world of the Gods. Its element is that of fire and its letter is 'I'.

Briah, meaning 'creation'. Represented by the letter H, and the element of water, where one idea might separate from the others although the world is still formless.

Yetzirah. Represented by the letter 'V' and the element of air. This is the concept of thought and imagination, with a level of consciousness that 'gives birth' to the physical.

The fourth and final world as called 'Assiah', which means 'to do'. It is represented by the letter H and stands for the element of Earth. This is about the physical world, the 'here and now'.'

ASTROLOGY AND THE ZODIAC

Technically speaking, the Zodiac is a division of space that is slotted into 12 equal segments that follow the path of the Sun during the 12 months of the year. It is a symbol in its own right as well as a 'home' for the other symbols that it encompasses.

But the zodiac is much more than this. It also encompasses the 12 constellations of stars that symbolize the different human personality types. Although the ancient Greeks and Romans coined the name 'Circle of Animals', the Zodiac also encompasses human forms too. If we assume that the starry constellations have been a part of the Universe that existed way before us, then its origins are open to conjecture. We do not know for certain from where it came, but it's generally believed to be in ancient Babylonia; their particular take on the concept used 18 segments. It was a Greek mathematician, Ptolemy, who defined the night skies in terms of the Zodiac. He wrote a work called *The Four Books*, which extrapolated the 12 constellations that we use, still, today.

Here are the basic meanings given to the signs of the Zodiac as they are personified, traditionally, in the Western discipline.

Egyptian Astrology uses a different 'set' of signs to match their deities. These are the Nile (Capricorn), Amon-Ra (Taurus), Mut (Scorpio), Geb (Aquarius), Osiris (Aries), Isis (Pisces), Thoth (Virgo), Horus (Libra), Anubis (Leo), Seth (Gemini), Bastet (Cancer) and Sekhmet (Sagittarius).

Hindu Astrology is also called Jyotisha. This is an amalgam of the Babylonian/Greek tradition along with ancient Vedic astronomical observance that marks propitious times in which to honour the Gods, sometimes using sacrificial rites. The names of the signs translate as follows: Mesa (Aries), Vrsabha (Taurus), Mithuna (Gemini), Karka (Cancer), Simha (Leo), Kanya (Virgo), Tula (Libra), Vrscika (Scorpio), Dhanusa (Sagittarius), Makara (Capricorn), Kumbha (Aquarius) and Mina (Pisces).

The Chinese Zodiac is, like Western astrology, based on a series of 12 signs. However, there the two methods change completely. The signs correspond to time: hours, days, weeks, years, etc., rather than astronomical bodies. The animals, real or imaginary, that star in this particular show are: Rat, Ox, Tiger, Rabbit, Dragon, Snake, Horse, Goat, Monkey, Rooster, Dog, Pig.

SYMBOLS OF THE OCCULT ❖ 63

GEMS AND STONES

The planet is full of stones, rocks, pebbles and the like. Although similar in substance, that charming little rock that you might have popped into your pocket, perhaps from the beach, is profoundly different to another, more valuable, lump that you might wear on your ring finger. The difference is in how we humans regard these intriguing rocks, some of them as ancient as the planet itself, which is, when you think about it, itself a lump of rock. It is easy to see why some rocks are free, whereas others are so expensive as to be priceless. It's to do with their sparkle and beauty as well as their strength. Ancient Egyptians were not alone in believing that precious gems held powerful forces. Important mummies were decked in them, just in the same way that latter-day crystal healers use them for their powers, whether perceived or otherwise. And who doesn't love a pretty crystal, even a cheap one?

The Breastplate of the High Priest

This is an extraordinary artefact of the Ancient World. The first such High Priest that wore 'the breastplate of righteousness and prophesy', known as the Essen, was Aaron, in 1200 BCE. The Breastplate sported 12 stones that are believed to have been sardius (possibly carnelian), topaz, garnet, emerald, sapphire, diamond, ligure (perhaps jacinth), agate, amethyst, beryl, onyx and jasper. Each of the gems were inscribed with the name of one of the twelve tribes of Israel. The gems were also a symbol of the 12 months of the year and the Zodiac.

There is a further mystery about the Breastplate – a mysterious relic called Urim and Thummim, still debated by scholars. Urim and Thummim was believed to have been put into the breastplate, possibly with the idea that the two were a means of asking God for guidance, a sort of cosmic lottery. A further theory is that 'urim' may mean 'guilty' and 'thummim', 'innocent'. Further symbolic meaning of this mystery still leaves questions unanswered.

Diamonds

Associated with strength and longevity, the Greek word for this most precious of gems is 'adamas', meaning 'tough' and 'untameable'. It is also very hard, so much so that during the age of Queen Elizabeth I, 'scribbling rings', featuring a sharply-pointed diamond ring, were quite the fashion; suitors would scratch the glass in windows with words or secret messages to be found by inamorata. Another of the symbolisms of the diamond is that they are neutral, able to absorb both good and bad energies. One such tale is of the Hope Diamond. Inaccurate rumours abound that it was stolen from the forehead of a statue of the goddess Sita. Over time, it fell into the hands of Marie Antoinette and Louis XVI, both of whom were beheaded. When it came into their possession, the banker Philip Hope and his nephew lost their fortunes. Where is it now? Safe in the vaults of the Smithsonian Institute.

Moonstone

The milky opalescence of this (semi-precious) gem really does seem to be made from the beams of a moon. It also has a witchy, spooky 'presence'. Once upon a time, this stone was called an 'astrion', a middle-english name for a star sapphire or precious stone that was believed to contain light from the stars, which could be gathered and collected for use. That the Moon waxes and wanes was, at one time, the source of the belief that the stone did the same thing. The psychic powers of the Moon is also believed to help humans tap into psychic powers, too.

Ruby

This precious gem is the personification of its colour – ruby red. This comes from the Latin, *rubens*, of the same meaning. In India, this is one of the most valuable of precious gems, called *ratnaraj*, or 'Lord of the Precious Stones'. The most valuable of such stones are known as 'brahmins', named after the high priest caste of India. Similarly, the title of the former Kings of Burma were called the 'Lords of the Rubies'. A ruby was said to have been set on the roof of the Temple of the Holy Grail so that the Knights could be guided by it. Hindu legends say that precious gem was able to light up the Underworld. Although the Ruby is undeniably a symbol of passion, it is also representative of the conscious control of the emotions, able to restrain lust and give clarity to the mind.

Opal

The beautiful colours that glimmer in this gem are there because there is a large amount of water that is retained by the silica from which the stone is made. This high water content means that the opal has a higher degree of sensitivity than any other precious gemstone, which means that it can be fragile and must to be kept, if possible, in a temperate environment. The changing colours of Opal gives the stone a distinct personality, which some believe is like a soul. There is a superstition that opal glows brighter if someone is about to die – perhaps the fever that sometimes comes with death is picked up by the stone? In other parts of the world, there is no such sadness around the gem. Amongst other attributes, the opal was said to give second sight, and psychic powers, to the owner… who may not appreciate such a gift!

Flint

If we call someone 'flinty', we mean that they are tough, not to be trifled with, in honour of the hard tough steeliness of the stone itself. Flint is a useful stone; along with steel, it can be used to start a fire. It was also used by Meolithic humans, used to make axeheads and the like. When, in the Middle Ages, we found these tools, we thought that they were the fossilised tongues of serpents; in addition, flint was mounted in silver and used as a charm to protect the cattle from bewitchment by malicious fairies and elves. The use of flint as a tool died away, however, as a way of sympathetic magic, shards of it were used to guard homes and outbuildings from lightning, fire and storms.

GEMS AND STONES

Bezoar Stone

This is a generic term for a 'stone' that is recovered from the innards of an animal, believed to have talismanic power from the animal itself. One of the most useful of stones was given the name of the Bezoar in Arabic; it means 'poison removing'. These stones were not found by one particular animal, but many. Not used much these days, the Bezoar stone emerged from cows, goats, camels and the like; images show that the 'stone' is actually a hardened mass of chewed hair that can be formed in the stomach of the animal or even a human. In the latter case, whilst a ruminant animal can expel the bezoar, this is trickier for a human, who may need surgery to remove the 'stone'.

Jet

This 'stone' is actually wood, rotted and compressed over not just thousands, but millions, of years. At the end of this long process the wood becomes as hard as a stone, able to be facetted and turned into a shiny black jewellery and the like. It was once found commonly in Whitby, a seaside town in Yorkshire, England, but supplies are now scarce to find and expensive. The dark black Jet became very fashionable when Queen Victoria ordered quantities of the stone when she was in mourning for her deceased husband, Prince Albert. It was said that jet could repel snakes, fix toothache and drive away demons. But the black symbolism of mourning still remains the single most well-known of all its efficacies, real or symbolic.

SYMBOLS OF WITCHES

Although Witches and their craft have never gone away, of late the interest in all things 'witchy' has become notably momentous. There are several ideas posited as to why this should be. The worldwide pandemic of 2020 may have contributed, as all of us had the time in the lockdowns to make potions and charms. More likely, though, is that a male-centred society, which had been 'in charge', has started at last to turn around, with a long-awaited feminine renaissance now loud and proud. Although some of the instruments of witchcraft are traditional, there are also new ideas about the Craft, and what it actually means to be a Witch in these interesting times. Generally, witches are women. Although there are still sabbaths during which witches meet with one another, these are also now to be found online.

Triquetra

This symbol, which literally means 'three-cornered' has been adopted by witches as a symbol of the three aspects of the goddess – maiden, mother, crone – but it is actually an ancient pattern that even pre-dates the Celts, who are usually most associated with the knot design. They placed significance on the number three, believing everything is born, dies and is reborn. In later years, it was also adopted as a Christian symbol depicting the Holy Trinity.

Athames & Bolines

An athame is a ceremonial knife, used by witches, which usually has a black handle. It is used to mark, for example, a magical circle, or to direct energy. It is not used to cut anything. The pointed shape of the object is a reminder of the fire principle. The boline is another ceremonial object, whose curved knife is shaped like the crescent moon, silver in colour. The handle is usually white. This tool can be used for cutting herbs for magical intent as well as for cooking.

Broomstick

Traditionally made by polished elm wood, the scarcity of the tree itself means that an alternative is needed. One contender might be ash, with its 'fingernails' of terminal buds, called 'witches fingers', although this tree is also in trouble. The 'broom' of the stick is from a plant, also called 'broom'. The act of sweeping was a sacred task in temples and other holy places. In Ancient Rome, special broomsticks were used to 'sweep away' any real or perceived negative influences after a child had been born.

Triple Goddess

There are many symbolic representations of the triple aspect of the Goddess, and many more aimed at witches. However, the one shown here is symbolically eloquent. It shows the circle, representing the full moon, flanked either side by the waxing and waning crescent moon. The symbol associates the Goddess with her moon as well as the changing of her three aspects as maiden, mother and crone. A moonstone gemstone set into the symbol as a necklet would add further meaning.

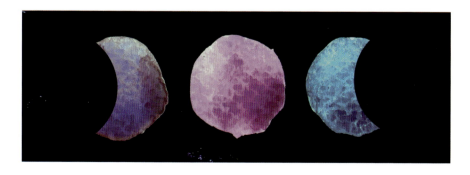

SYMBOLS OF WITCHES

SYMBOLS OF DRUIDRY

What, exactly, is a druid, and what is Druidry? The origins of latter-day Druidry evolved from the priests of the Iron Age, who, it is said, were known as druids. The word, 'druid', stems from a much older word (possibly Sanskrit) meaning 'tree', specifically, the oak. At the heart of the latter-day druids is a veneration for the natural world and everything in it, including human beings as a part of the ecosystem, not separate or superior as is sometimes the case in other religions. In the 18th century one Iolo Morganwg emerged as the exponent for a druidic revival. It is impossible to pinpoint exactly what the early druids believed; most of their knowledge was given hand to mouth, and the coming of Christianity meant that the druids were allegedly massacred by the Romans. Now, though, Druidry is recognised as a religion in the UK. Many of the implements and physical symbols of Druidry are shared by those of Wiccan allegiance, and there are also similar thoughts in regard to the veneration of the natural world.

The Awen

This word, from the Welsh language, means 'essence' or 'inspiration'. It is often used at the beginning and end of ceremonies, related to a Brecon symbol, the Triban, also a reminder of a Hindu deity, Shiva, in the ancient Sanskrit tongue. Each of the three 'dots' of the symbol have meanings. These include 'past, present and future', the 'three pillars of wisdom', or 'love, truth and knowledge'. As a meditative focus, the three syllables are chanted slowly, out loud, three times, allowing the sound to resonate. You may choose your own three symbols, too.

The Tree of Life

This is a stylized image of a tree, representing the oak, which symbolises strength, longevity, respect for the natural world and all who live in it. With great age comes wisdom, and this is also part of the symbolism of the Tree of Life. Because trees were on the planet long before human beings, the symbol is also a reminder of this, as well as the idea that trees were, and are, our 'ancestors'. In this, we see similarities with the Native American peoples who have the same ideas, that is, being a part of nature and the natural world.

SYMBOLS OF DRUIDRY

The Acorn

This little 'nut', the seed of the mighty oak tree, symbolizes growth and the prospect of unlimited potential. This is not exclusive only to those of the druidic persuasion. The acorn has to lay dormant in the autumn and winter until it is ready to start growing in the spring, a symbol of patience and the need to rest and think things through before we are ready to ask. The oak and the acorn together are symbolic of the cyclical nature of life.

The Green Man

A relatively new idea, the Green Man image that we see most frequently was brought forward at sometime in the 1930s, although the idea behind it was much older. This is a popular motif, a spooky-looking man, made of leaves and foliage that, ideally, hide the figure. The technical terminology for this powerful symbol is called a 'foliate head', a Disgorging Head, and even the The 'Bloodsucker Head'. The figure can also be traced back to India, travelling through the Arab empire and then on to Christian Europe. Incidentally, Green Woman as a reminder of the natural world is becoming more popular, as of course it should be.

IMAGINARY ANIMALS

As though real animals, birds, insects and the like were not enough, we humans also like designing imaginary ones too. Why is this? As a creative and imaginative species, we humans just can't resist the urge to design myriad ideas, including animals. Some of these creatures are indigenous to certain countries and areas, and others might be the product of the fossils of real creatures not yet identified. All of them, somewhere along the line, were devised for a reason that we do not know. Some of them are to be seen in the Heraldic world, others in fantasy films and books.

The Griffin

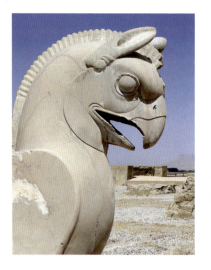

Also called Gryphon, Gryphes, Grypho, and more. This legendary creature has the body, tail and back legs of a lion, the head and wings of an eagle and with talons on its front legs. A powerful, majestic creature, the job of the Griffin was to guard priceless treasures. It was Pliny the Elder that told us that Griffins had wings and long ears, whereas Apollonius of Tyana said that they did not have wings, only short, webbed feet, which presumably means that they couldn't fly for very long. That ancient peoples believed that these creatures were real is certain. The Persian name for them was *shirdal*, meaning 'lion eagle'.

Cyclops

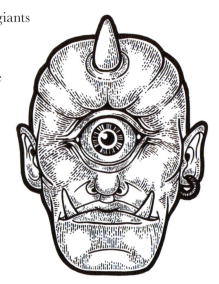

In Greek mythology, this was a race of giants that had one single eye in its forehead. In Homer's book, *The Odyssey*, these terrifying creatures, of which there were three, were cast as shepherds, whereas other accounts say that they were gods. As a movie star, the Cyclops is perennially popular, with numerous films from all over the globe (Croatia, Japan, Bulgaria, USA, to name just a few). They also star in the Dungeons and Dragons games, contemporary music (The Libertines) and also in art (Odilon Redon).

Tengu

A facet of the Shinto belief, Tengu are thought to be a mischievous beings, someone who was arrogant and proud in a former life. Said to be expert horse riders, it was the Tengu that taught the military arts to one of the Japanese heroes, Yoshitsune. The Tengu are believed to live in trees in remote mountainous areas, and would appear to be male, as there seems to be no mention of any female tengu.

Unicorns

An ancient imaginary animal, the Unicorn has friends and believers all over the world, especially with little girls. It first came to our human attention in the artworks of ancient Mesopotamia from whence it was referred to in the myths of India, China and then to most of the world. The Unicorn looks like a horse with a single horn on its head, and is usually white. In the Greek bestiary, known as the Physiologus, comes the notion that the animal can be tamed only by a virgin girl. Once this happens, so the story goes, the Unicorn leaps into her lap, and then she suckles it and leads it to the local palace.

Despite the strange story, the Unicorn is a symbolism of chastity and salvation. The beauty of the Unicorn means that it is well-known, seen in religious symbolism as well as in art galleries, movies and the like.

Dragons

A symbol, for many cultures, of power, found throughout the world. A perfect description of this imaginary creature can be found in Switzerland, on the Dragon Path on Mount Pilatus (also known as the Dragon Mountain):

Dragons are subterranean, winged, smoke-and-fire-breathing creatures, hybrid go-betweens in a magical bond between Heaven and the Underworld, where they guard secret treasures and reign over fires and concealed palaces.

It seems as though we humans *need* these creatures; we imagined them and then gave them life. Dragons come in many guises and varied cultures, always a sign of power and potency as well as protection. In Celtic mythology, the Dragon is the guardian of treasures, often concealed underground. The Dragon, in China, is symbolic of strength and magnanimity. Other symbolic meanings for this fabulous creature incude transformation, good luck and wisdom.

Banshee

In Irish folklore, the Banshee (in Irish, *Bean Sidhe*) is a female spirit, who heralds the death of a family member by screaming, wailing, shrieking and/or 'keening' (this is a high-pitched wailing sound), usually in the hours of the night. Unlikely to be seen, nevertheless, in 1437 the Scottish King James is purported to have been approached by a Banshee. These creatures come in three forms; as a young woman, as a middle-aged woman, and as the crone. As well as this she can be disguised as a washerwoman, rinsing blood from the clothes of the deceased. Spoiler alert: there is a possibility that the Banshees are not actually supernatural beings, but 'keeners', women that sing funeral songs. The word, 'keening', means to wail in grief for a deceased person.

Yeti (and Sasquatch)

Also known as The Abominable Snowman, this is an ape-like creature, well-built and much taller and wider than even a tall man. It has shaggy fur and a lean, muscular ape-like body, and some accounts describe large, sharp teeth. Although there are claims from people who have had sightings of such a creature, nevertheless it is still part of the ancient folklore of the Himalayan people. Most of the tales of the Yeti see him as a figure of danger, a warning not to stray too far away in the snowy wastes. In the folklore of the Native Peoples in the Pacific North West is found a similar creature, Sasquatch, also known as Big Foot, close in comparison, although several thousands of miles apart. Perhaps they are cousins? Big Foot is also symbolic of the need to stay safe in dangerous conditions, in mountainous and other remote areas.

Mermaids

The myth of the mermaid has very ancient origins, said to date from the Assyrian civilisation, around 1000 BCE. The origin story goes that the Goddess, Atargatis, Great Mother of the Gods, accidentally killed her lover (who was mortal) and in her grief, turned into a mermaid. As anyone who has seen a mermaid can attest, they are very beautiful. They also like to lounge around on rocks, admiring themselves in a mirror and constantly messing with their hair. Mermaids also feature in the Greek story of the Odyssey, in which the Sirens' song was so beautiful that the sailors had close their ears to the music lest they drown in the attempt to get to the rock, possibly to say hello, but possibly for some other reason. The Mermaid, with her beauty and allure, is a symbol of sexual frustration.

Sphynx

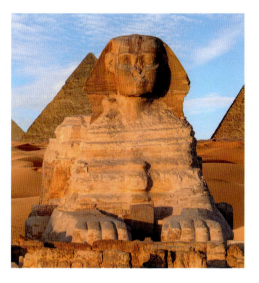

In Greek mythology, the Sphynx is something to stay clear of, given that it is a treacherous and merciless being. It has the head of a woman, the haunches of a lion, and the wings of a bird. The Sphinx is a gate-keeper, challenging those who encounter to answer a riddle. If the hapless traveler cannot answer, the Sphynx devours them. In Eqyptian mythology, though, the Sphynx is a man, without wings, a guardian of the Pharoah, often seen flanking the entrance to a temple. The most well-known example is the Great Sphynx of Giza, which dates to somewhere between 2600–2500 BCE. The use of the statue is unknown, its meaning a riddle in itself.

Faun

In Roman and Greek mythology, a Faun is a creature that is part human and part goat, very similar to the Greek Satyr. The name came about from Faunus, the name of a deity associated with fields, forests, and other natural places. Clearly the Greek god, Pan, with his goat-like horns, hooves, and pan pipes, is a Faun. The name, Pan, also lends its name to 'pandemic', 'pangalactic' and 'pandemonium'. In the film/books of Narnia, Mr Tumnus, half goat and half man, is a kindly example of a Faun. In general, the Faun is a symbol of the forces of nature, fertility, and more than a little sexuality. Apart from the kindly Mr Faunus, most fauns are not to be reckoned with or trusted, much like the weather, a changeable mischief-maker.

IMAGINARY ANIMALS ❖ 95

THE SYMBOLISM OF ANIMALS

From the world of imaginary animals, we now turn our attention to the real ones. We often forget that we humans are also animals, and that we have many of the same interests: food, safety, sex, even happiness (although possibly not religion). Some believe that our liking for religion elevates us from the animal kingdom, whereas others believe that it could be our downfall. The animals that we know from our life on earth have a wealth of rich and interesting symbols to think about. Depictions of animals, whether wild or domesticated, have rich symbolism for us to uncover.

Ant

For some, such a tiny creature might seem to be significant. That would be a big mistake! The ant was one of the teachers of one of the wisest kings, Solomon. Given its well-known habit of self-inflicted hard work, it is a symbol of industry. The teamwork of ants is notorious, many of the small creatures working together as one in order to achieve a goal. This is an example of the saying 'the sum of the parts being greater than the whole'. While some aspire to the hard work of the ant, others can see its efforts as a symbol for the amassing of material goods.

Bee

Who doesn't love a bee? Now, as in the ancient world, the insect is important because of the honey that it makes, which is symbolically loaded as a symbol of sweetness as well as preservation. As well as this, the bee is a sign of mutual co-operation. One of the symbols of the Greek goddess, Aphrodite, was a golden honeycomb, and it was believed that the souls of her priestesses inhabited the bodies of bees. These Priestesses were called Melissae, a popular name for girls whether or not they like honey. The male counterpoint to the Priestesses were called Essenes, meaning 'drones', which was also the name for the eunuchs.

Cat

For some reason, even the most ordinary of cats has a mystique about it. It is somehow mysterious, out and about, and screeching to her contempories and the Moon. Although we love our domestic cats, it was the ancient Egyptians that regarded the cat so highly that it was revered as a deity – the cat goddess, Bast. This was especially so if a cat had fur of three different colours or eyes of different shades. The Goddess Artemis, Goddess of the Hunt, is also associated with cats, whose hunting skills she shared. Buddhists, though, were not so keen. Because the cat was absent at the death and therefore the resurrection of the Buddha, it is viewed with suspicion. Although the 'Lucky Black Cat' is an archetype for westerners, black cats are supposed to be able to transform themselves into djinn, able to shape-shift and even possess humans.

Dog

'Fido', a traditional name for a dog (if rarely used these days) shares the same root as 'fidelity' and indeed, this is a trait of most dogs. For thousands of years, dog and man have happily lived and worked together, with a close bond of mutual understanding. A dog will stay faithful to the end and also beyond; the dog is a psychopomp, guiding the soul of its master or mistress to the next world. Because the dog is known to have extraordinary powers of scent, a skill which is denied to us in such precision, we have accorded the animal with powers of second sight and even psychic abilities. The legendary hunting prowess of dogs is reminded in myths, such as the Hounds of Annwyn who, in Norse mythology, hunted with the God, Odin. The Goddess of Death, Hecate, also had her hounds.

100 ❖ SYMBOLS

Goat

A symbol of lust and procreation, one of the more interesting mythical beings of ancient Egypt was the Goat of Mendes, also known as Baphomet. This deity was worshipped in a rite in which slaves copulated with goats, a ritual intended to honour the power of nature. The Ancient Greeks identified the Goat as Pan, the God of Nature. Later, with the coming of Christianity, the old Gods and their interesting practices were personified as evil. A 'Scapegoat' is still used when someone takes the blame, but the origin of this can be found in the Old Testament of the Christian faith. Two goats were liberated, one set free and the other killed. The remaining goat, symbolically laden with the sins of the people, was usually pushed from a great height, human sins forgiven for the time being.

Hare

A nocturnal creature not often seen, the hare is a symbol of the Moon, hidden wisdom, intuition, secrecy and the Goddess archetype. In some parts of the world the shape of the hare can be seen in the moon's face. The animal is noted for its fertility, and it is this that is simplified and somewhat 'cleaned up', with chocolate eggs given at Easter, often unknowingly in honour of a springtime goddess, Oestre. This pre-Christian tradition has never been satisfactorily explained away. Also, any animal that is eaten usually means that it has sacred status. Three running hares, joined at the ears, is a mysterious ancient symbol that appears in Buddhist caves over 2500 years old as well as in latter-day jewellery. This might well be a further iteration of the Tripple Goddess.

Horse

This creature, for thousands of years, has been of important spiritual, mythical and symbolic meaning. It has a close partnership with humankind, not only as a beast of burden and as a way of travel. Our love of its intelligence and noble nature means it is seen in palaeolithic cave drawings, for instance at Lascaux, created some 30,000 years ago. Symbolic of the Sun and of fire, the horse is also an emblem of the Moon, and water, too, because the Gods of the Oceans ride on its back. In common with the dog, the horse is a psychopomp, guiding the souls of the dead to the journey of the next life. Because a horse can be ridden for miles, it is also a symbol of freedom. A white horse is a sign of magical meaning as well as spirituality. A black horse is a symbol of death, often seen in funeral carriages.

Mouse

It may be a surprise that such a small creature is one of the forms taken by the God, Apollo, in his aspect as both destroyer and creator. In Europe, the mouse was at one time the symbol of a soul leaving a body. The soul is said to escape through the mouth as the dying person took his last breath. There are even said to be eye-witness reports of this event. In Christian symbolism, the mouse is said to be a bad influence as it gnawed at the base of the cross, therefore undermining such an important symbol of the faith. In the Hindu pantheon, the mouse appears with the great elephant-headed Ganesha as 'riding' the God. This is a symbol of humility.

BIRDS

Older, even, than humankind, birds are the ultimate messengers of the Gods. Because they can fly, they can carry messages from the spiritual realms. We have been fascinated by birds for generations, as testified, for example, at the prehistoric cave paintings at Lascaux in France. One such bird effigy, named 'Death of the Bird Man', tells us that it is possible that there was a bird-cult as long ago as the paleolithic era. Birds, too, are the carriers of messages and omens, and this idea holds fast throughout the planet. In Greek, 'bird' and 'omen' have the same meaning. Most civilizations had their augurs, people who knew how to interpret the meaning of the birds. The word 'inauguration' comes from the Latin, 'augury'.

Crane

Fossil remnants tell us that the Crane has been on this planet for 10 million years. The bird itself has a long lifespan (50 years or more) so it stands to reason that it is a symbol of longevity. The God, Hermes/Mercury, said to have invented the alphabet by observing the wings of the bird. The letters were carried in a crane skin bag, which is also the title of a book by Robert Graves. For the Greeks, the bird was a symbol of the sun, and the God, Apollo, disguised himself as the bird when he visited Earth. The Crane is also a psychopomp, guiding the souls of the dead. The bird's dance represents the power of flight and the arrival of human souls in the Lands of the Immortals.

Dove

The Dove is a universal symbol of peace, generally viewed as a feminine trait. When Noah needed to determine how far he was from land, the bird returned with an olive branch, a symbol of peace and also a useful marker of the end of the long journey. In the USA, the dove is a covert symbol, reasoning femininity balancing the overtly masculine eagle. A symbol also of love, doves cuddle together on wedding cards as a symbol of it. For the Greeks, the Priestesses at the Temple at Dodona were named 'doves'. The birds that perched in the sacred oak there were believed to have the powers of speech. For Christians, Mary the Virgin is often paired with a dove, a symbol of the Holy Spirit. At Mecca, there are specific perching places for the birds. However, the dove can be a warning of disaster, too. In Wales, UK, where once there where many coal mines, the sight of a dove is a warning of disaster. There is a tale from the 19th century that 300 miners refused to work when a dove appeared.

Magpie

In Italian, the word for magpie 'gazza' means 'chatterer' and, in English, 'pie' stands for 'pied', which means 'black and white'. So, the name between the two languages is, effectively, 'Black and White Chatterer'. Known for its attraction to shiny objects, the Magpie is not only a thief but a hoarder, and this, as well as its black and white markings, made it a symbol of the devil for some Christians. However, the bird is innocent, just doing its own thing… or is it? That the bird is highly intelligent and able to mimic our human words and sounds can be alarming. In Scotland, it is said that the bird has 'the devil in his tongue'. In Japan, it was believed that if a husband gave his wife a mirror, then it was possible that the mirror could turn into a magpie, able to spy on behalf of the husband.

Owl

In Italian, 'strega' or 'strix' means 'witch'. And here is a hint as to the meaning of this bird. Because of its nocturnal nature, the owl can access secrets, occult knowledge and the like. Because of this, owl is often seen, in museums and galleries, with the goddess, Athene, as a symbol of wisdom. The owl can swivel its head 270 degrees, meaning that its eyes really can see round the back of its head. Like traditional witches, owls are also solitary creatures. Although they come together to breed, the birds separate from one another when the babies are ready to fly. The silent wing feathers mean that the bird cannot be heard. The superpowers of the eyes as well as the feathers makes the bird an impressive hunter; Pliny noted the 'striges', women that could transform themselves into birds of prey. The owl and the Moon together are symbols of feminine power and prophesy.

Raven

If the average IQ for a human is around the 100 mark, the average raven clocks in at a massive 138. This bird has superb linguistic skills, can mimic human words, solve problems (such as dropping stones into a glass of water to raise the height so the bird can drink). This intelligence is the hallmark of a trickster. In Norse mythology, it was the ravens, Hugin and Munin, who flew back to the God, Odin, each day, and whispered into his ears the various doings of humankind. The bird, with its stern countenance and gleaming black feathers, is a harbinger of death, as in the Morrigan, the Battle Goddess of Celtic myth. The ravens at the Tower of London have been there for over a thousand years, because of a legend that the country would be safe from invaders for as long as the ravens remained. In the Second World War, Churchill arranged that ravens were imported from Wales to London to make sure that the country stayed safe.

OTHERWORLDLY ENTITIES

As well as mythical animals and real animals, we have the symbolism of otherworldly entities. These creatures evoke fear or awe, according to the meaning that humans ascribe to them. As such, they are ultimately symbols of other worlds that we wish to know more about or, in the case of hell, avoid.

Angels

The idea of these heavenly creatures – and their hellish counterparts – are believed to have been extant for at least three thousand years, mentioned in the Hebrew scriptures as well as in Zoroastrianism too. Whether or not these beings are real, or purported to be, is as yet unknown, and on a planet in which not everyone could read or write, we would only have had the images of angels to speculate upon, no eye-witness sightings to ponder upon – except, of course, in the many images and statues made by people. If angels did not exist, then we would probably need to invent them. Whether or not they are 'real' is, in fact, not the point. The sculpture, The Angel of the North, in the UK, said to be the largest such statue in the world, was based, not on an idealized creature but on a human; this means that viewers are able to freely attach their own ideas to the sculpture, the idea of the artist, Anthony Gormley.

Demons

More symbolic riches can be found in the ranks of our demons. As the counterparts of angels, demons can lure us with false promises, making our resolve to be better human beings end up in the hand cart to hell.

In Pan, a Nature God, there are also connotations of the Demon, Satan, as effectively the same entity. In his earlier guise, Lucifer was the best and brightest and best of all, called the 'Morning Star'. It was the founders of the medieval church that tinkered with the idea, making him into the 'rebel angel', the frightening and horrific entity that is perceived today.

Ghosts

The idea of ghosts is fearless for some, petrifying for others, and business for the psychics that purport to provide a go-between for them. Whether or not they are real is not necessarily relevant. According to popular folklore, those who say that they have actually seen a ghost tell us that the apparition can look like a clear impression of the deceased or perhaps something more nebulous. In general, the belief in ghosts is based on a very ancient idea that the human spirit is separable from the body, with an existence after the body is relinquished. Although many are sceptical, the idea of a ghost is so enduring that perhaps there is truth in their existence!

Ghouls

The origins of this word derive from ancient Arabic, a word meaning 'to seize'. They are demonic beings, noted for their habit of lurking around graveyards and similar lonely places, described by Edgar Allan Poe as '…

neither man nor woman, neither brute nor human'. They were also said to ride on dogs, set fires at night and lure lone travellers into becoming horribly lost. Ghouls are not exclusive to Arabic folklore, either. In the Tamil mythos of India, the 'pey' would seem to be a close cousin, a creature with shaggy hair and a penchant for hanging around during battles, waiting to lap up the blood of the dead and dying.

THE WRITTEN WORD AND THE SPOKEN SOUND

What would we do without words? If you think of any kind of alphabet, the letters that make up that jumble of words are actually a series of magical ciphers, one of the best gifts that the Gods could ever bestow upon us. The series of squiggles that you see here contain many of the secrets of the Universe. Imagine a world without these squiggles! The journey from a sound, said out loud, to a written symbol, is a mysterious one, and no matter which language we speak, it is likely that the provenance of these words were given by divine intervention; for example, the god Thoth, for ancient Egyptians, Hermes in the Greek tradition, and Odin in the Northern mythos. Not so very long ago, reading and writing were only for the priestly classes, because with these gifts came the power of knowledge. The ability to understand the alphabet is a great treasure, when you think about it. Here, we show just a little of these ancient and magical words and sounds.

Abracadabra

Generally used by entertaining magic acts, the Abracadabra is a very ancient word, believed to have been inspired by the Aramaic *Avra Kedabra* – which means ' I Create as I Speak'. Other theories as to the meaning of this word include an idea that might have been in honour of the word, *Abraxas*. Another notion is that it was derived from a Hebrew phrase, *Abreq ad Habara*, meaning 'hurl your thunderbolt until death'. A further idea is that it is from the Aramaic *Abhadda Kedabhra*, meaning 'disappear as this word'. The latter makes a lot of sense! Finally, there are those that say the first letters of the word might be a cipher for the initials of three Hebrew words that mean Father, Ghost and Holy Spirit.

Runes

Used in both ritual and secular ways, the runes are the oldest script symbols in countries such as Scandinavia and Germany. The word, 'rune', means in old Norse or English 'secret' or 'mystery'. The Eddas, ancient Scandinavian poems, tell how the God, Odin, brought the runes to humankind after hanging from an ash tree for nine days until he could see the symbols clearly in the water below. The shapes of the runes are distinctive, made of upright parts (staves) and diagonal lines. This is because they were originally scored in wood, believed to have been from the wood of fruit trees. The Elder Futhark is the most often seen of several different systems, and it comprises 24 symbols. Each of these contains a small universe of meaning, carrying within it a sound, a shape, a name and a mystical meaning. This is completed by the Wyrd rune, a blank rune of mystery.

Ogham Tree Alphabet

This set of sacred symbols is named for the Irish Celtic God, Ogma, who is said to have invented the alphabet and who was also the deity of poetry and learning. Ogma means 'language'. There are 15 characters, all of which are associated with trees or shrubs; hence the collection of letters is called letters called The Tree Alphabet. Just like this book, the 'letters' are broken down into five sets, the whole called a 'grove'. This alphabet is not only a collection of specific trees, but also the sum of the knowledge that is contained in each tree too. Each small part contributes to the greater whole; it is no surprise then that the words for 'knowledge' and 'wood' sound the same. The order of the trees goes like so:

TREE

1. Birch *Beth*
2. Rowan *Luis*
3. Alder *Fearn*
4. Willow *Saille*
5. Ash *Nuin*
6. Hawthorn *Huath*
7. Oak *Diur*
8. Holly *Tinne*
9. Hazel *Coll*
10. Apple *Quert*
11. Vine *Muin*
12. Ivy *Gort*
13. Reed *Ngetel*
14. Blackthorn *Straif*
15. Elder *Ruis*
16. Elm *Ailm*
17. Gorse *On*
18. Heather *Ur*

Aum

This is a living symbol that exists, in varying forms and names, in Hinduism, Buddhism, Taoism and others, as well as to adherents of Yoga. It translates as something like 'Amem' (Hebrew) or 'Awen' (of contemporary Druidry). The Aum is the living and breathing symbol of The Word that was present at the Creation of the Universe. In the Yoga Sutras of Patanjali, this idea is expressed as 'God's Voice is Aum'. When used at the beginning and end of the prayer, the person who chants the word becomes a part of the three manifestations of God: Brahma, Vishnu and Shiva.

SYMBOLS IN NATURE

Imagine how early humans regarded nature. As well as its beauty, there must have been fear, too; the elements, impossible to second guess, changing at the drop of rain or tornado – or tsunami. The symbols that we note in the landscape reach out to us in the common purpose of climbing them, walking them, admiring them, wherever we are on this planet.

The Skies

To look up at the skies is a shared experience, the symbols of clouds and other phenomena clear to read, common ground for people in a similar vicinity. It is reasonable to think that the 'The Heavens' – 'up there' –were observed to be the abode of an all-pervasive power, both generous in helping us grow food to eat and water to drink; and it is equally reasonable that if that power turns dark, drowning crops and destroying homes, that we would think that we had done something wrong.

The Sun/Kolovrat

It is a little-known fact that the Sun, generally believed to be a male force relation to fire, male energy and vitality, is also seen in many beliefs as female. Her many names include Sunna (German), Sol (Norwegian) Amaretasu Omikame (Japan) and Sulis (Celtic). The glory of this star, though, makes it the absolute physical manifestation of a Supreme Being, the 'Eye of God'. To our ancestors, when the Sun tipped over the edge of the sky on the Western horizon, they believed that it had disappeared into the Land of the Dead; logic also believed that, because of this, the Sun could be the harbinger not only of life, but also of death.

The Moon

Illuminated at night by the light of the Sun, it carries all the positive – and negative – female traits. Without the light of the Sun, none of the Planets in our solar system would be illuminated and life, as we understand it, would be obsolete. Therefore, the Earth and the Moon have a symbolic allegiance. As a mirror of the Sun, the Moon relies on instinct; the Owl, sharing the same symbolic space as the Moon, is regarded as a bird of knowledge, hidden concepts and secrecy. In simpler days, women would menstruate and ovulate at the same time. However, artificial light and other man-made environments means that this is not always the case.

The Milky Way

Our galaxy – our home – has many names; not all of them use the idea of 'milk' in the terminology, but many do! In Latin, it is the *Vial Lactia*; in Greek, *Galaxias*; in Irish, it is 'Way of the White Cow'. The number of stars in our galaxy really is astronomical; between 200 billion and 400 billion. This mass of stars is the edge-on part of a sparkling, spiral-shape

of a cascading river of diamonds. It's not at all surprising that the Milky Way has captured our collective imaginations for millenia. Indigenous Americans see it as a pathway to another world; the Samoyed call it the Spine of the Sky. Wherever you are, one clear evening, make a point of dodging artificial light and see it for yourself.

Mountain

Wherever your mountain is, in whichever part of the world, whether one of the highest or one of a more modest scale, the symbolism of this natural and beautiful feature of the landscape tells a story of inspiration, renewal, creativity and vision. To climb a mountain is to push beyond normal life in exchange for a moment of wonder and brilliance, closer to the realms of the Gods, far away in both height and the difficulty in attaining such a wonder. People who are lucky enough to live in, or close to, mountains have a great fondness for them; the film, 'The Englishman Who Went Up A Hill But Came Down A Mountain' is a great example of this, when the status of the local mountainous feature is questioned. An inch or so can make a crucial difference!

River

Water is, of course, essential to all life on earth, and a river resonates with our most primal instincts. It is a source of beauty, enchantment and adventure. To sit for just a little while can carry away our worries and anxieties along with the water. In Mark Twain's stories of Huckleberry Finn, the river is a symbol of freedom; however, the natural world can be hazardous and frightening too, an analogy for life. Rivers are also a lyrical symbol of the passing of time as well as a more prosaic meaning, equated with goods and the notion of commerce. A flowing river is a natural highway, taking us into physical, as well as metaphorical, horizons.

Lake

So similar, but so very different from the river, the stillness of the lake provides a rich tapestry for stories. A lake can be the giver of fertility as well a symbol of death. A lake can be unfathomably deep, a mystery; the Lady of the Lake, in the Arthurian tales, is an enchantress who is said to live in a castle beneath the lake, and also gives him the magical sword, Excalibur. A still lake is akin to a mirror, symbolizing the depths of a reality that we cannot comprehend. When light travels through water, the water slows down, changing reflections, enabling us to see things in a different way.

Ice

In the world of symbols, water is never simply just 'frozen ice'. It is rigidity and frigidity, cold, hard, angry, even jealous. It is the absence of human feeling and love, instead a symbol of the nastiness or hatred and deliberate destruction. However, there are some good points about ice! Given the right circumstances, i.e. symbolic warmth as well as the real kind, it is possible, underneath that coldness and clarity, ice is able to transform very quickly, which means that it is adaptable to the point of obliteration of the self.

PLANTS

Until you start to notice plants, be they either native or exotic, it can be easy to forget just how important their symbolic usefulness is and how much we rely on them every day, either medicinally, or otherwise. Plants, too, are able to show an alternative view of conventional reality. Psychotropic plants, such as peyote and marijuana, can induce dreams and visions, a gateway to another dimension that is said by some to be the realm of the gods. Taking these drugs, for many, is a rite of passage, guided by the shaman or curandera. Although opium, cannabis and various magic mushrooms are available to the curious traveller, alcohol, too, is a drug, often misused, any more subtle use of its symbolic meaning damaged, simply because of its universality.

Amaranth

In the Victorian era, this plant was very popular, its long strands of tiny red flowers a symbol of immortality, and therefore also used in mourning. The Goddess of the Amaranth had a temple dedicated to the plant, Artemis Amaranthia. Amaranth is indigenous to Mesoamerica, a seed similar to buckwheat, and very nutritious. The Aztecs used the plant as a symbol of immortality, constructing huge statues of their God, Huitzilopochtli, once upon a time covered in blood as a human sacrifice, but covered in honey, with the seeds pressed into the statue, during less violent times. In the same way as the Host is offered in a Catholic church, the honeyed seeds were shared as they would be in the Sacrament.

Basil

There are many different kinds of basil, but all are fragrant. The leaves are said to have magical powers, used in love potions as well as a divinatory tool to gauge the likelihood of people having a happy marriage – or not. Holy Basil is part of the Hindu tradition. A Goddess, Tulsi, was seduced by the God, Vishnu. When she realised what had happened she was ashamed, and killed herself. A remorseful Vishnu made Tulsi a symbol of faithfulness. The Holy Basil that sprang underneath her feet was named for her, and the Sanskrit name is how this basil got its name. The word itself has origins that are both Greek and Roman, in both, the meaning of them is in the word 'royal'. The evil basilisk – a legendary reptile – is said to be counteracted by the herb that gives it its name. Holy water containing any kind of basil is said to be the most effective in exorcisms.

Garlic

This plant has strong antiseptic qualities and is renowned for warding off disease of many kinds. Symbolically, it is a symbol that is second to none, a talisman to ward off evil vampires; in order to do the job, the vampire needs to be tied to the bed, so bear that in mind! According to the Talmud, garlic increases male potency. However, in the festivals that were sacred to Demeter and Athene, women ate garlic as a way of making sexual abstinence easier, perhaps because of the odour. At one time, the whole garlic family (including onions and chives) was believed to be a snake repellent. Garlic is renowned the world over, still of use to us thousands of years later. At one time, brides carried bouquets of garlic as a symbol of good luck, but this practice seems to have died out in favour of far prettier nosegays.

Hemp

A universal moniker for the many names of cannabis, the species smoked in countries way before the Conquistadors discovered tobacco were Cannabis sativa and indica. As is the case with popular items of all kinds, there are several folk names attached to this plant, including *bhang* or *ganga* (Sanskrit) and *hashish* (the original word for 'assassin'). The the native South American name of marijuana was interpreted as 'Mary Jane'. Everywhere, though, it is called 'weed'. Hemp makes for a very useful fabric, strong and resilient, but its use as a ritual substance stretches back to neolithic times. The Mahayana Buddhist tradition reveres the plant as sacred because of the Buddha, whose 'one seed a day' regime was believed to bring him to his exhalted status.

Juniper

This plant, in pre-Christian times, was believed to harbour spirits within it, so the plant itself was treated with due reverence. Because the berries take three years to ripen, they are a symbol of patience. The aromatic fragrance of the wood was used by Buddhist monks in their temples, and even today the smoke is used as an aid to meditation. Because they grow in lone and windswept places, juniper is a symbol of resistance. Also, there is some truth in the old wives' tale of inducing abortion by using a hot bath and a bottle of gin. Unpleasant, and thankfully longer in use, this old saying does have some credence to it, as the berries can cause uterine contractions. Therefore, gin is contraindicated for pregnant women.

Mistletoe

Also known as the Sacred Bough in mythology, this is a mysterious creature. It grows only in the sky, meant never to touch the ground, so symbolizes the heavens. It is propagated by birds, themselves symbols of the gods, and the pearly opaque 'berries' are symbols of fertility, as they resemble drops of semen. It was probably this that caused the idea of the 'kiss under the mistletoe' to start. Traditionally, the mistletoe is supposed to be found on oak trees, but in fact this is rare; it's far more likely to be hanging in the messy branches of old apple trees. At one time people believed that lightning caused the mistletoe to grow, but this is not the case. Birds, notably the mistle thrush, excretes the seed as she eats. Druids, traditionally, harvest mistletoe using a golden sickle (representing the Sun). The association with Christmas time and the mistletoe is uncomfortable for some devout Christians, as it is a powerful reminder of pre-Christian beliefs. Despite this, it is sometimes called *Lignum Sanctae Crucis* because of the bizarre notion that upon the cross on which the Christ was crucified was a mistletoe.

Lily

One of the most important plant symbols on this planet, the lily, when white, is a symbol of innocence and virginity; when the angel Gabriel came to Mary, it was a white lily that he held. Also, the phallic-looking pistils, spreading its shower of pollen, is also a mark of reproduction. In just one flower we see virginity, fertility and the Mother. The name of the Babylonian Goddess, Lilith, is derived from the name. The flower is sacred to the goddess Astarte, whose name was given to 'easter', so when bunches

of the flower are given during the festival, we are inadvertently nodding obeisance to this goddess. This flower is also seen in symbols of royalty, notably in France, where it is still a mark of nobility.

Lotus

Although generally not found in American or European gardens, the lotus, nevertheless, is renowned for its beauty as well as its habits, in the symbolism of China and India. A sensuous bloom with perfect petals, the lotus rises in murky and malodorous swampy places, reaching for the Sun, symbolizing the triumph of Spirit over Matter, hence a reminder of a person's journey to enlightenment. Further, as night falls, the lotus retreats back into the murk from which it came. For the ancient Egyptians, this was seen as a sign of death and rebirth. The eight petals symbolize the four cardinal directions, the ones inbetween, and the eight directions of the Universe. The Buddha is often found sitting cross-legged within a background of lotus petals, detached from the material world.

TREES

So prevalent, reliable and useful; without them, as humans, we are doomed. The uses that trees give us are far-reaching and often surprising. For example the Linden Tree (Tilia) is used to calm a fever, make elaborately delicate carvings, footwear and more. In terms of symbolism, a tree combines all elements; water (in its sap), earth (in its roots); its branches are in the air, and the tree can also be used to make fire. Also, trees process carbon dioxide. Our ancestors were tree-worshippers, and although you might not realize it, so are we. You don't need to hug trees to appreciate them. But it helps! Trees were on this planet way before humankind and we have a lot to be thankful for when looking at their symbolism. It was a tree that Christ was said to have hung from, rather than the traditional cross. The world over, trees give us food, shelter, medicine, the warmth of a fire and, of course, beauty.

Ash

Believed by some to have been the first tree ever created, it is impossible to know whether or not this is correct. What we do know is that this tree is known as the Queen of the Forest, associated with all the feminine qualities of silver, water and the Moon. Yggdrasil, the 'World Tree' of Norse mythology is an ash, its roots stretching to the very heart of the Earth, and its branches up into the heavens, sheltering the entire universe within her woody arms. Sacred oaths were made on spears of its wood, because its wood was strong and unlikely to split. Because the tree can have male and female flowers on the same tree, it is a symbol of the union of opposites. Older trees sometimes split to reveal a chasm, the hole used to pass babies through in order to protect them, leaving small tokens for the tree under the branches.

Oak

The counterpoint to ash, the oak is the King of the Forest, an accolade throughout all the temperate world. A tree of great longevity which can stand for over a thousand years, the famous Oak Grove of the Greeks gave its home to the birds that carried messages from the gods themselves. The ship, the Argo of Greek myth, was cut from oak. Before manmade places of worship became the norm, it was trees that we worshipped. The oak was, and is, of sacred status; the name, Duir, is of the oak, and the word 'door' has the same origin. The botanical name of the oak is *robor*, the same root as 'robust'. An even more unusual use for oak trees is in the oak gall. These are little 'wooden' balls from a parasitic wasp which are used to make a black, indelible ink, used not only in the American Declaration of Independence but also in the Magna Carta.

Apple Tree

The mythical Isle of Avalon, which means 'orchard', is derived from the ancient Welsh word for 'apple'. It is also the name of the resting place of the Celtic kings, including Arthur. The apple, like the ash, symbolizes the World Tree and as such the axis of the Universe. The time of the apple harvest coincides with Halloween, or the older pre-Christian Samhain. At this time the apple has an important place to play in rituals and divinatory practices. The apple also has a magical symbol hidden in it. Cut the fruit in half around the circumference, and you will find five pips inside, forming a five-pointed star within. When Eve gave Adam the apple, she also gave him the pentagram inside. This is a symbol of possibilities, opened only when the pips were revealed. The apple is not the only fruit that does this.

Cedar

Long lived, large, imposing, dark; the cedar, in particular the Cedar of Lebanon, is a symbol of longevity. The incorruptibility of the wood was used in the building of the Temple in Jerusalem. As with all evergreens, the Cedar is symbolic of immortality. The Romans carved effigies of the gods from the wood of the cedar, the beautiful scent making them even more special. Cedarwood resin was used in the tombs of the Egyptians. The Assyrians believed that the patterns on the bark held the secret and sacred names of the gods, and the egg-shaped cones were used as charms to repel demons. The funeral cult of the 18th century Britain meant that cedars, with their dark, imposing trunks and fragrant scent, became popular in graveyards, some of them still towering over the gravestones.

Elder

Part tree and part shrub, the elder is prolific, and the more they are cut down the stronger they seem to get. A height of up to 20 or more metres is possible, and a girth of two metres is unusual but not impossible. The elder is presided over by the Elder Mother, also known as Freya, in the Norse mythos as well as in Native American stories. This tree is believed to have all the characteristics of the mother, kind but firm, but not to be messed with. In as much as the berries have been used for at least 5,000 years as a tonic, it has been found that the natural antibiotics in those berries are indeed efficacious for a number of applications such as influenza. This tree is also believed to be a doorway for elemental beings, such as fairies and spirits, and its wood, in the same way, is (apparently) used for the broomsticks of witches.

Hazel

The Celts believed that the hazel was the ultimate Tree of Knowledge, aligned with the tale of the Salmon of Wisdom, which acquired its knowledge by eating the nuts of the hazel tree, of which there were nine. The name, 'coll', which means 'hazel', was also the name of the Kings of Ireland, once upon a time. The tree was so sacred that it was punishable by death to cut it down. However, hazel is so useful in coppicing new shoots for varied uses, such as in weaving or dowsing, that this rule has been ignored with no discernible harm done. Nevertheless, selecting a wand for the purposes of dowsing is still carried out in a careful and ritual way by some dowsers, with penalties for harming the tree. The wand needs to be chosen at dawn on a Wednesday, as the God of the Hazel, aka the Norse god, Woten, also ruled that day.

Olive Tree

This tree, which prefers Mediterranean climes, is a universal symbol of peace and hope. When Noah sent a dove from the Ark to see if land was close, it was a sprig of greenery – believed to be of the olive – that gave the good news that home was close. Because olive oil has high nutritional value, it was considered a sacred plant, and it was a punishment to harm it in any way (except, one would imagine, an exemption for eating it). Because the tree grows to a good age, they are a symbol of longevity. In Islam, the olive is an important and blessed tree, its fruit mentioned seven times in the Quran. Each leaf is said to have one of the names of God inscribed upon it. Also, the olive is seen as a symbol of light because of the olive oil that used to burn in lamps.

Yew

One of the most long-living trees, the way that the yew grows – often with ungainly branches – means that it is tricky to determine their age without specialist equipment. However, we know that these trees can grow for at least 5,000 years and possibly more. Often seen in churchyards, the reason for this can be laid at the feet of the early Christians. Effectively, they carried out a marketing campaign that allied the ancient tree with the new religion, and as the tree was already a symbol of both longevity, rebirth and death, it worked. The branches of the tree, in rain, glows a reddish-brown a little like blood. Although poisonous to the point of deadly, nevertheless there are compounds in the tree that are useful in some cancer treatments. The genus of the tree, *Taxus*, lends its name to one of those treatments. It is called 'Tamoxifen'.

CURIOSITIES

Here, we include a brief roundup of some of the interesting, odd, and often unusual symbols that are tucked away in strange places, with some of their uses.

Apotropaic Objects

These are objects that hold magical significance, usually by the owner of the house. Generally found in houses that are of 19th century or older, such objects were squirrelled out of sight in walls, floorboards, within the chimney breast and in other cunning places. In a world largely built on superstition, rituals that protected the home, family and livestock were important. Such objects included horseshoes, the heart of an animal (likely to be sacrificial), single shoes and other various items. In addition, so called 'witches' bottles' that featured a face or other motif were also popular, filled with iron nails, sharp pins, nail clipping and urine were used to harm the witch, albeit remotely.

Cimaruta

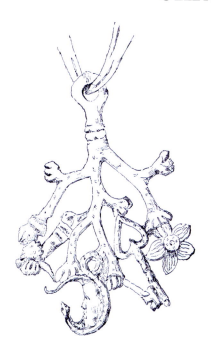

This is an amulet that is made in the form of a sprig of the herb, rue. It is generally rendered in silver as a feminine charm, a token of the Goddess, with three or more charms hanging in its branches. Said to be traced back for several centuries, its provenance is said to be Etruscan. The charms can be chosen from several different alternatives, such a crescent moon, a key, and stars. It is also known as a Witch Charm, although its popularity seems to have waned somewhat in recent years.

Tomoe

The name of this symbol means 'circle' and is comprised of three comma-like shapes in the form of a spiral. Once upon a time, it was a part of the heraldry of the Japanese Samurai and is also a symbol of both Buddhist and Shinto faiths. The Tomoe looks similar to the yin-yang symbol, and shares a similar meaning. The three 'flames' are representations of the earth, the heavens, and of humanity.

CURIOSITIES ❖ 147

Pueblo Zia Sun Symbol

An ancient and magical symbol of the Pueblo Indians, this sacred symbol comprises a circle with four sets of four stripes (see opposite). The whole is a Sun symbol, and the Zia is the name of the Sun itself. Four is a sacred number for these people, who see it as the four seasons and directions, with the fifth element containing the whole. Often seen on pottery, it is also to be observed on the flag of New Mexico.

Seal of Shamash

This was the symbol, used as a sign of the Sun God, in Mesopotamia. It was used for several centuries, both before and after 1,000 BCE, in the general area of the Euphrates. The foundation of this symbol is very simple but also profound because of it. The center is a dot surrounded by a circle, with four rays that look very much like a child's version of the Sun. Sometimes, the simplest ideas work best!

148   SYMBOLS

Question Mark

Sometimes the most obvious symbols are those that we use every day, and this is no exception. Or is it? Look more closely and you will see that the 'wave' is an emblem of the area between the spiritual and material worlds, i.e. the space between what may be a possibility and what is real. The dot, or *bindhu* (see page 11), is a symbol of the seed of potential, or actual reality.

Torii

A symbol of Japan, the Torii is a gate or a doorway, but one of sacred intent. This opening belongs to the Shinto religion. The Torii marks a place that is liminal, that is, a place that marks something significant such as between this world and the next, the material from the spiritual, the sacred from the profane. It is believed that the name of this sacred gateway encompass the Shinto words for 'bird' and 'place'. Birds, of course, can go wherever they like, even, perhaps, even from this world to the next.

Flower of Life

A symbol from sacred geometry, the Flower of Life is a pattern of overlapping circles that form 'petals' in their intersections. As a pattern it has a long history due to its roots in mathematics, with it showing up in various cultures throughout the world including Ancient Egypt and within the Roman Empire. Leonardo da Vinci incorporated some of the shapes from sacred geometry into his artworks. While it is a two-dimensional shape, meditating on it allows the viewer to access different dimensions and to see the inter-connected nature of the Universe. In this way, it is similar to a mandala.

Caduceus

This is a rod or staff – or a wand – surmounted by two wings. A pair of snakes twine up the staff, making a figure of eight shape. This is a very ancient symbol. Its earliest recorded sighting is believed to some 2,600 years ago, on the goblet of the King of Lagash. However, this symbol, despite its great age, is very much still in use as a sign of healing and medicine. The first known physician, Aesclepius, used the Caduceus as an attribute, because of the wand and the wings, to be able to use the destructive nature of the serpents to restore health, a practice which is still in use today, albeit without the snakes.

Omphalos

A Greek word, meaning 'navel'. Not only restricted to that country, because the navel is seen to be the centre of the human body and therefore in contact with the life force of the mother, the omphalos therefore, symbolically connects the Earth with the same force that is generated by the God. The same concept can be found in the Lingham (India) as well as the World Tree. The stone on which the Arc of the Covenant rested on, is also an Omphalos.

Persian Rugs

Anyone who has a Persian rug – even a cheap one – is stepping on ancient stories and symbols. Two such rugs, which might look identical to the naked eye, will be ever so slightly different and the reason for this is wonderful. The weavers, down the centuries, weave in a deliberate mistake, an acknowledgment that only Allah is perfect. Effectively, the rug is a perfect mistake. Does this mean that it is doubly perfect?

Rebis

This is just one of many symbols that represent the idea of the hermaphrodite. Also called the Twofold Matter, the Rebis is a perfection of being, comprised by a perfect balance of opposites. The yab-yum, in India, has the same idea, as does the yin-yang of Chinese tradition. The oval shape that frames the pair looks like an egg, which is a symbol of the cosmos and of new potential.

INDEX

A

Abracadabra 118

acorns 84

Albert, Prince 72

Alfa Romeo 7–9, 40

Altars 19

Amaranth 129

Angel of the North 108

Angels 108, 109

Antoinette, Marie 65

Ants 98, 99

apotropaic Objects 143

Apple Tree 138

arcs 14

Ark of the Covenant 22, 154

Ash 136, 137

astrology 60–1

Athame 76

Aum 115

Awen 83

B

Banshees 91

basil 130

Beckoning Cat 38, 39

Bees 98

Bezoar stone 72

Big Foot 92

birds 104–8

Boline 76

Breastplate of the High Priest 65

Bride's Chair 50

broomsticks 79

Buddhism 34, 35, 98, 100, 101, 133, 135, 146

C

Caduceus 152

Cats 100

Cedar 139

charges 45

Chi Ro 24

Chimney Sweep 40, 41

Chinese Zodiac 61

Christianity 16, 18, 19, 22, 23, 24, 101, 102, 105, 134, 143

Cimaruta 146

circles 14

Coleman, Pamela 54

colours 44

Cranes 104

Crosses 15

Cyclops 88

D

Demons 112

diagonals 18

diamonds 65

Dogs 100

dots 11

Doves 105

dragons 45, 61, 90, 91

Druze Star 29

E

Egyptian astrology 60

Elder 139

Elizabeth 1st, Queen 65

F

Fauns 94, 95

flint 71

Flower of Life 152

47th Problem of Euclid 50

Four Books, The (Ptolemy) 60

four leaved clover 40

Fulu 30, 31

G

garlic 130, 131

Ghosts 112

Ghouls 114

Goats 101

Gormley, Anthony 108

Graves, Robert 104

Green Man 84, 85

Griffins 88

H

Hares 101

Hazel 140, 141

hemp 133

heraldic symbols 42–5

High Priestess (Tarot card) 54

Hindu astrology 60

Hinduism 11, 25, 26, 27, 34, 60, 68, 98, 102, 115, 130

Hitchcock, Alfred 18

Homer 88

Hope Diamond 65

horizontal lines 15

Horses 102

horseshoes 38

I

IHS 22, 23

Islam 16, 31, 98, 104, 105, 141, 154

INDEX ❖ 157

J

Jainism 11

jet 72

Judaism 22, 31, 58–9, 65, 101, 108, 139

juniper 133

K

Kabbalah 58, 59

Khanda 24

L

lakes 128

Laughing Buddha 34, 35

level and plumbline 48

lines 15

lily 134

lotus 135

Louis 16th, King 65

Lover (Tarot card) 55

lozenges 16, 45

M

Magpies 105

Mermaids 92, 93

Mice 102, 103

Milky Way 125

Mistletoe 134

Moon 125

moonstones 68

Morganwg, Iolo 81

mountains 126, 127

Murti 27

O

Oak 138

'Odyssey, The' (Homer) 88, 92

Ogham Tree Alphabet 120, 121

Olive Tree 141

Omphalos 154

opal 71

Owls 106

P

Persian rugs 154

plants 129–35

Pliny the Elder 88, 106

Ptolemy 60

Pueblo Zia Sun 148, 149

Q

question mark 150

R

Ravens 106

Rebis 155

rivers 127

roses 9–10

Rowling, J.K. 18
rubies 68
Rudraksha 27
Runes 118, 119

S

Sasquatch 92
Seal of Shamash 148
Shintoism 29, 89, 146, 150
Sikhism 24
skies 124
space 11
Sphynx 95
squares 16
Sri Yantra 25
Sun 124
Sun, The (Tarot card) 54
Supreme Polarity symbol 33
Swastika 25

T

Taoism 31, 32, 33
Tarot cards 54–7
Tengu 89
Tomoe 146, 147
Torii 150, 151
Tree of Life 83
trees 136–43

triangles 18, 50
Triple Goddess 78, 79, 101
Twain, Mark 127

U

Unicorns 89
United States Dollar Bill 51

V

vertical lines 15
Vesica Piscis 16, 45, 56
Victoria, Queen 72
World (Tarot card) 55
Wrens 108

Y

Yantra 34
Yazidis 31
Yeti 92
Yew Tree 143
Yin Yang symbol 33
yorishiro 29
zigzags 19

Z

Zodiac 60–1
Zoroastrianism 108

PICTURE CREDITS

ARK: Krikkiat / Shutterstock.com

GANESHA: Vinayak Jagtap / Shutterstock.com

DRUZE STAR: Fakhad Veronika / Shutterstock.com

YAZIDI: Ruslan Harutyunov / Shutterstock.com

THE SUN TAROT CARD: bigjom jom / Shutterstock.com

ZODIAC: Nina Drozdowa / Shutterstock.com

BEZOAR STONES: rchat / Shutterstock.com

FAUN: Juan Pablo Chachi / Shutterstock.com

ANGEL: lucarista / Shutterstock.com

HEMP: Leitenberger Photography / Shutterstock.com

All other images courtesy of Shutterstock.

ACKNOWLEDGEMENTS

Many thanks go to my enthusiastic friends and helpers who made great suggestions. In addition, huge thanks to Tania Ahsan, John Turing and the team at Arcturus for giving me the opportunity to revel in the beautiful playground of Symbols – this has been a blast!